DROPPING THE BALL

──◆──

Baseball's Troubles and How We Can
and Must Solve Them

Dave Winfield

with Michael Levin

SCRIBNER

New York London Toronto Sydney

SCRIBNER
1230 Avenue of the Americas
New York, NY 10020

SCRIBNER and design are trademarks of Macmillan Library Reference USA, Inc.,
used under license by Simon & Schuster, the publisher of this work.

For information about special discounts for bulk purchases,
please contact Simon & Schuster Special Sales:
1-800-456-6798 or business@simonandschuster.com

Text set in Bembo

Manufactured in the United States of America

1   3   5   7   9   10   8   6   4   2

Library of Congress Cataloging-in-Publication Data

Winfield, Dave, date.
Dropping the ball : baseball's troubles and how we can and must solve them /
by Dave Winfield with Michael Levin.
      p.   cm.
1. Baseball—United States. I. Levin, Michael Graubart. II. Title.

GV863.A1W56 2007
796.357—dc22   2006101385

ISBN-13: 978-1-4165-3448-8
ISBN-10: 1-4165-3448-2

In Recognition

To my immediate family, Tonya, Arielle, David, and Shanel, for understanding my love for the game and supporting me in everything I do.

To my mother, Arline V. Winfield, for her unfailing support. She watched every game she could that her sons played. It made me who I am today.

To my brother Steve, my best friend and teammate of so many years, who has dedicated his life to teaching kids baseball.

To the Parks and Recreation Department of St. Paul, Minnesota, that has been the best for so many years and is number one in the nation today.

To Kirby Puckett, the best friend and teammate a guy could have. You made a great impact on so many, but you left us too soon.

To Dorothy Bowen. Your help and support in my early San Diego days helped me stay grounded and get my foundation off the ground. You've left a positive impact on so many.

To John "Buck" O'Neil. Your life was one worth living. You became baseball's greatest contemporary ambassador. Your love for others and your positive outlook on life were truly worthy of the Hall of Fame. We'll miss you, my friend.

To John Moores, for bringing me back to MLB, where I've gained the insight and motivation to write this book.

To my coauthor, Michael Levin. You've been the consummate teammate through the whole process of writing this book. You've been great to work with from the very first outline and title selection. From the beginning your love and knowledge of the game shone through, hence our ideas flourished and our exchanges were lively. I'd say my 2006 draft pick for a coauthor was an extremely successful one.

Contents

DROPPING THE BALL

The Game I Love Is Hurting

Opening day, 2012.

A group of kids, fresh from a morning of pickup games at their neighborhood baseball complex (built by a partnership of sports, local business, and government interests), arrives at the major league ballpark early enough to sit in the box seats and watch batting practice. The stars of the game take time to give them some baseball cards, sign a few autographs, offer encouragement and some tips about how to make it to the majors, and even toss a few balls the kids' way. The kids—and their parents—also meet some MLB alumni who serve as team ambassadors and who answer questions and share memories (and some autographs, too) with the fans.

As batting practice gives way to fielding practice, the stands begin to fill with fans of all racial and ethnic backgrounds, as culturally diverse as the players on the field, thanks to Major League Baseball's outreach and marketing programs aimed at minority communities. A few of those fans are enjoying their choice of hot dogs, sushi, and other ethnically diverse foods from the food stands, which now also offer healthy and vegetarian alternatives. In the upper deck, parents are teaching their kids how to score the game between innings at the park's interactive game areas and museums. The parents are also thinking back to that period in baseball history when the game on the field kept giving way to strikes, lockouts, ownership collusion, and owners deliberately fielding weak (and inexpensive) teams, maximizing revenue by minimizing salaries. Thanks to the commissioner and Major League Baseball working in cooperation with the Players Association, all that divisiveness is a thing of the past. The commissioner's office and Players Association have a feeling for the game, and its players are on the same page.

The owners and the Players Association worked out a mechanism that rewards top players and free agents for working within the baseball campaign as well as for performing community work—even after they've gotten their huge, multiyear contracts. Of course, players still change teams, but the system now provides incentives for players to remain in one city for many years, long enough for fans to get to know and relate to their team and players—or even for their entire careers, like a Tony Gwynn, a Kirby Puckett, or a George Brett. And Major League Baseball, MLB.com, marketing, international business groups, and the Players Association made an agreement to promote individual players and not just teams or the overall game, so the fans know much more about the new arrivals to their favorite teams.

The chasm between players and fans has vanished, as players demonstrate a newfound respect for their fans and for the game, and take a much more active role in their communities, visiting schools, hospitals, and service clubs like never before. As a result, players have regained respect and adoration from their fans. The players and their union have become much more aware of the players' responsibilities as role models in society (for which players now receive recognition and distinction) and, to that end, have crafted a successful drug-prevention program that includes drug testing and has all but eliminated steroids, amphetamines, and other performance-enhancing drugs from the game. Thanks to the cooperation between Major League Baseball and the Players Trust (an arm of the Players Association), the perception—and the reality—is that the game has truly been cleaned up, and the baseball players' ratings have skyrocketed as a result. The ballpark is using its boardrooms and facilities to assist community-based programs and partnerships that further baseball, the youth, and the community in general.

The World Baseball Classic has become an unqualified success as a platform to embrace worldwide baseball enthusiasts from Africa, China, and beyond. The ethnic, cultural, and racial diversity on the field is also reflected in the fan base. Baseball has become aware that diversity is a business imperative, and has acted accordingly. While continuing their avid pursuit of baseball players in Latin America, Australia, Japan, and China, the owners have created a system that makes it economically, socially, and politically intelligent to develop homegrown baseball players, of all races and socioeconomic levels, through such initiatives as the Urban Youth Academy, which began in Compton, California, in 2006, and has expanded and begun to bear fruit.

In 2012, kids of all backgrounds have access to the same high-quality tryouts, baseball camps, travel leagues, tournaments, showcase games, scout games, trainers, coaches, and even sports psychologists. No longer do kids who are potential five-tool ballplayers (those with all of the abilities that baseball prizes: hit for average, hit for power, run, throw, and field) fall way behind because they lack access to the training facilities, big league exposure, and coaching that gives other kids knowledge of the nuances of the game vital to career success. Coaching clinics, provided by each ball club in Major League Baseball and conducted by dedicated people with a renewed love, understanding, and respect for the game, are held nationwide. How far you can go is no longer dictated by where you come from or what kind of resources your family has.

As a result, it has become just as economically rewarding to develop prospects in the inner cities of the United States as it is in the villages of the Dominican Republic. In 2012, when any young player enters the clubhouse of his first major league team, he is likely to see others of his racial or ethnic background.

Baseball is enjoying such a great resurgence that kids in their teens continue to play on high school and college campuses, where the girls are just as interested in the baseball players as they are in the football players, basketball players, and skateboarders. And the casual fan can name as many noted college programs and coaches in baseball as he can in basketball.

Sounds farfetched? It shouldn't.

In this book, I want to share my observations about the current state of baseball, why the game *appears,* by most standards, to be in robust health but is in fact subtly declining in importance to Americans, especially African Americans, and share my ideas for turning the trend around. This book will tell you how baseball can go from good to great, and how the game's industry can be all it can be.

I love the game of baseball and I revere its place in both American history and modern society as a teacher of values and life skills and outdoor fun and exercise, as well as its place in the history of race relations. I come from a time when there was respect for the records we hold dear and when role models were plentiful. As baseball combs the world, from Latin America to Europe to Japan and Australia for new prospects, new audiences, and new sources of revenue, the game cannot afford to forget the fans and the prospects here at home. The path to the top is much different than it once was. I will explore the connections among the social and economic issues, the people side and the business side of baseball, and discuss how baseball can reach its full potential.

Despite the record attendance figures and huge labor contracts, the game has diminished in popularity over the last thirty years due to many factors, some subtle and others quite obvious. Each of its many constituencies, from the commissioner's office to the owners to the players and even the fans, have lost sight of what makes baseball unique. I want this book to serve as a critique of baseball, and to provide a guiding light for those who have the fondest love for the game. I've applied some vision, suggesting some bold strokes and initiatives to produce major change.

These thoughts are coming from the heart of an insider, one who played and loved the game as a seven-time Gold Glove winner, with over three thousand hits, a World Series winner, and a member of the Baseball Hall of Fame. I've been asked: Why risk being shot down or criticized? I say, "Why not me, why not now? No one else is offering solutions—we have entered an awareness phase of our plight, but action is next." My objective is to move beyond criticism to offer well-founded and well-researched answers, directions, and advice. I'd like to provide an introspective guide to the present and the future of the game, and offer a manifesto for change.

A lot has to change in the way baseball is marketed, played, and appreciated in order for the game to regain its luster. I will take issue with many of the practices employed by the various constituencies described in the book. I'll discuss simple timeworn practices that have been lost or forgotten. But I will always remain positive, upbeat, and hopeful that once those responsible for baseball's success realize what needs to be done, they will act quickly to preserve our true national pastime and bring it into the twenty-first century.

Baseball has lost its central position in the hearts and minds of sports fans in America, and I want to explain what this decline in baseball's importance, particularly to African American fans and young people, means to me. Then I will focus on each of baseball's constituencies to address the issues everyone in and around the game needs to consider. I will suggest ways in which each of those groups can bring baseball back to the fore. My final chapter, "Baseball in the Twenty-first Century," will offer my vision for how the game can resume that rightful place at the center of our sporting life, but only if all the constituencies pull their weight.

I remember a sign that George Steinbrenner had on his desk in New York: LEAD, FOLLOW, OR GET OUT OF THE WAY. Take your choice. I've made my decision to lead, and I'm hoping to ignite some action and perhaps bring baseball back to its former glory.

As a retired player who has loved the game since I was eight years old, and as a baseball executive for the San Diego Padres, I have the ear of the leading figures in the game, from the commissioner's office to the Players Association to the corporate community leaders, team owners, and media, right down to the coaches in Little League. I possess an intense passion to get these ideas into public debate. It has been more than a decade since I retired from the game. When I played, and also while in retirement, I have privately documented and discussed scores of ways in which baseball could improve itself. This book is the product of twenty years in the major leagues and another decade of thought and research.

The time has come to deliver a message of utmost importance to our society as a whole, not just to those who love the game of baseball. I will share with you what can and must be done to reverse the trends that have maligned the sport I love. I want the book to accomplish an extremely important goal: to kindle a national, ongoing debate about the future of the game, and to incite change.

Everyone can see and feel the changes in baseball—few of which have been any good—but not many people can sense when or why the game changed. Everyone has an opinion about what's wrong, but no one has offered a cure. The sports talk shows speak authoritatively on a few issues and can easily identify the topic du jour, but they are chock-full of fluff. And that's as deep as it goes. I want to go much deeper than that. I want to discuss where the game has been, where it is now, where it's headed if we do nothing about the problems baseball faces, and where the game can go if we understand what's possible.

If you look at baseball's recent history—from labor struggles to collusion on free agents' salaries, from strikes to steroids, from congressional hearings to HGH and amphetamines—you might get the sense that the game was doing everything in its power to destroy its own credibility and importance. Indeed, baseball—its players and its leadership—has slipped over the decades from its preeminent position as the national pastime to its current position as simply one more entertainment option for Americans. People used to feel a sense of ownership about baseball. Pro basketball belonged to the NBA, pro football to the NFL, college basketball to the NCAA. But baseball belonged to the *people*.

That's changing—for myriad reasons we'll discuss and debate. A growing number of baseball seasons interrupted or even a World Series wiped out by strikes hasn't helped our image. The period when the owners were found guilty of colluding to keep down the salaries of top free-agent stars didn't help much, either. Baseball's attitude toward the steroid problem—denial, followed by a quick fix, followed by more denial, then much berating in congressional inquiries—has been a disgrace.

Yes, the turnstiles are spinning at record numbers, a new era of labor peace has ushered in bigger and bigger contracts, and new ballparks continue to be built, which means that people still want to come out and see the games. But I know it's changed when I see that today's fathers can't teach their kids baseball because so many of them never even played themselves. Nevertheless, baseball remains popular. Of course, so does World Wrestling Entertainment, which no one believes is anything but scripted.

I love the game of baseball. Always have, always will. I was a pretty good athlete in my youth, blessed with an early love of the game and some great coaching, and I became the only individual to have been drafted by four teams in three different professional sports leagues—the Minnesota Vikings of the NFL, the Atlanta Hawks of the NBA, the Utah Stars of the old American Basketball Association, and the San Diego Padres. I could have chosen any sport, and I chose baseball.

People often ask me why. I reply that there were baseball fields near my home in St. Paul, Minnesota, and there were coaches who knew and could teach the game and its values: hard work, teamwork, winning. The game was fun because I was taught how to keep growing and succeeding. It's a hard game that many quit because they don't learn how to improve. But with great coaching, both individuals and teams can achieve success. As a boy, I'd dream of accomplishments on the diamond: "That was the hardest ball I ever hit!" and "I struck him out with the side-arm pitch!" or "That play deep in the hole was the best play I ever made!" Every day, I wanted to come back to do it better.

Why not football? Well, the idea of getting my body banged up by guys even larger than me every fall and winter Sunday didn't appeal to me. Just ask most former college or NFL running backs or linemen coping with all manner of aches and pains if they now believe that they made the right career choice. Many of the pro football players of my youth who were my heroes are no longer with us. And the ones whose bodies have never recovered from those violent collisions will tell you, "Man, I should have played baseball."

I like basketball and excelled at it in my years at the University of Minnesota. One on one, five on five—if you've got the physical tools, heart, and endurance, it's a great game as well. I had fun playing basketball, but baseball has always been *the* game. In fact, I used the training and mental techniques I gained in sports such as basketball to improve in my sport of choice. A lot of people, myself included, think that baseball is a harder game to learn and to play than any other. It is truly a skill sport—talent alone doesn't cut it, and size does not ensure success, either. Scientifically, it encompasses biomechanics, physics, and aerodynamics, to name just a few.

Baseball is also an instinct sport: It takes intelligence and planning—not just reacting. It takes time and effort, practice and good coaching, to hone those instincts so that you can understand what you have to do, including the proper exploitation of opponent's weaknesses. The skills include how to initiate action, how to respond to events, how to lay down a bunt or hit behind the runner (the kinds of skills that don't show up on *SportsCenter*).

Above all, players need to know how to ask and answer the key baseball questions: "What if?" What if he hits it to me? Where do I throw? Who do I back up? All the things that people don't see that are going through a good player's mind long before the pitch. That's why I love the game so much: Because it's a cerebral experience as much as it is a physical one. You're not constantly moving, but you have to always be thinking.

Consider that college and even high school players often make the leap to the NBA or the NFL and become starters, and even standouts, in their first year in the pros. But that's not the case in baseball. Even outstanding players who have excelled at every level of the game from the time they were in T-ball spend several years in the minor leagues honing their skills before they are ready for prime time. Think back to Michael Jordan and his baseball odyssey. If Jordan, arguably the greatest basketball player of all time, could barely hit a minor league curve ball, that ought to give you some indication of the skill required in baseball. And it's a game you have to continue playing: Unlike riding a bicycle, you can't stop for years and hope to pick up where you left off.

It's unfortunate that many kids today are not permitted to play multiple sports in high school and college, which would help them determine which one they truly want to play. The trend in society toward specialization has reached the world of competitive sports: Coaches expect you—at a very young age—to focus on one sport, *their* sport, in and out of season. If you don't follow their rules, you don't play, because coaches, too, are feeling the pressure to win. This stifles the growth of young athletes and means that they may not end up in the sport for which they are best suited, because competency and enjoyment in a sport grows with time.

Playing multiple sports helped me with versatility. Playing basketball and football in high school and college taught me life lessons about confidence, overcoming obstacles, endurance, running and jumping, competition and teamwork, and it kept me from burning out on one sport, as is often the case today. Playing three sports with different practice routines, and cross-training in the off-season, I developed muscles and attributes beyond those which baseball required. I also met new people, traveled to different places, and competed in a wide variety of arenas. This was a great experience for me, and it would be for any young person. I'm afraid today's generation of specialized high school—and even adolescent—athletes are missing out on those opportunities for growth.

As the father of three children, one of whom is a twelve-year-old Little Leaguer, I'm acutely aware of the pressures on young athletes—limited time, unlimited expectations from teammates, coaches, and parents, especially when your last name is Winfield. I won't lie—I want my son to love the game of baseball, just as I always have. That's a major reason for my writing this book—so that my son, and yours, can have a chance to learn and love what, in my eyes, is the greatest game.

Baseball is probably the most cerebral sport there is, relying on intellect and experience more than any other game. The lessons from baseball are endless—it takes more than talent to play the game well. You can't be good without the proper coaching of techniques. You can't learn the nuances of the game on your own. It takes enormous focus, study, and flexibility. You've got to have multiple capabilities—you're not performing the same skill over and over, like a football linebacker or a hockey goalie. In addition, the baseball schedule is longer and more grueling than any other in professional sports. We play approximately twice as many regular season games as they do in the NBA and a dozen times as many games as does the NFL. Our road trips are longer, and our games themselves take longer to play. Baseball today requires a player to be intensely fit so as to survive the rigors of the long season, the physical demands of the game, and the endless travel, not to mention the emotional demands of the media, the fans, and the business side of the game.

W. P. Kinsella, the author of the novel *Shoeless Joe,* which was adapted for the movie *Field of Dreams,* wrote that the physical action that takes place over a three-hour baseball game could be compressed into five brief minutes. The rest of the time is taken up, for the fans as well as for the players, managers, and coaches, imagining what might happen next: what pitch might be thrown, what defensive adjustment might prove harmful or beneficial, where and how the ball might be put in play, what the runners will do. Baseball is a thinking person's game, and that's part of why I love it so much.

And I've been thinking a lot about baseball lately. If I don't say or do something soon, I'm afraid it will evolve into a sport and a business that I will not recognize, like, or even respect. At some point in the recent past, baseball went from being a sport to being a form of entertainment—to being a business that has neglected its customers, the people who love the game. It's difficult to determine when and how this tipping point occurred, and it didn't occur on just one front. In recent years, industry meetings have revealed to me that the regressive statistics and trends have been brewing for more than a decade.

If baseball's a *sport,* then we have certain expectations. When you play a sport, you do your best and give your best at all times. You expect to win and you do everything you can to help your team. You run out grounders, even when it seems overwhelmingly certain that you'll be thrown out at first base. You hit behind the runner to move him over and put him in scoring position, even though the potential RBI won't be reflected in your own personal statistics. You lay down a bunt when necessary and you give yourself up for the team, for the greater goal of winning. You play to improve and enjoy, and a lot of life lessons are learned as a result.

But if baseball is *entertainment,* the fundamentals of the game matter less. Even winning doesn't matter as much if you feel entitled to a good salary with benefits, perks, bling, and TV coverage. A rookie makes more than the bonus a player wins for winning the World Series, so imagine the temptation to not play to his best ability. It's no longer about the joy of playing and winning, now it's all about the hype. It's about getting on *SportsCenter* so as to increase your chances of prevailing in contract negotiations and product endorsements.

Every player hopes to see himself on TV while having a sense of entitlement and keeping a distance between himself and the fans. Players and agents are more cognizant of performing actions that get them recognized. They're not always thinking, "What can I do for my team?" Instead, they're often thinking, "How can I become a star?" They're not hitting for the situation, playing solid defense, throwing out runners, or running out every play. Instead, there's a huge concern about individual glory and statistics.

In an era of free agency, it's harder to think in terms of the team concept. You often don't know your teammates very well (which results in a lack of team chemistry) because no one stays on the same team very long. It's harder to be on the same page with your teammates when the clubhouse has a revolving door. Remember the Tigers or Dodgers infield of the eighties? Or, if your memory goes further back, the Cubs or Twins infield of the sixties? The idea of an infield or outfield staying together for years is an anachronism today. Don't get me wrong: Good teams and good players will always emerge. But it's different. Players, managers, and fans don't know what to expect from year to year.

Who's influencing the players to think more about themselves and less about their teams? The agents play an important role in this process. They tell their player-clients, "If you can put these numbers up this year, I can get this kind of money for you. I can compare you with such and such a player." But the three-run homers that players shoot for today have nothing to do with thinking in terms of the "team." That's one reason why I say the game I love is hurting.

Another issue is the responsibility of the players to the fans. If baseball is a sport, then players are inevitably role models for kids. But if baseball is entertainment, or strictly business, the expectations for players descend to the level of what society expects from entertainers. You don't expect Madonna or Tom Cruise to sign autographs for kids before or after a performance. And you don't expect to get to the movie theater an hour early and watch Brad Pitt practice his acting drills before signing movie stubs for a group of moviegoers. Instead, these stars usually ply their trade and then go about their business, normally fleeing from the media and the paparazzi, leaving the fans to admire them only on the red carpet or at award shows.

Ballplayers are under more intense pressure and constant scrutiny than most public figures. When I played, the New York media were demanding enough. But now you've got twenty-four-hour sports talk radio, heated arguments on a thousand and one cable TV sports talk shows, the Internet, a million commentators taking every side of an issue, not necessarily because they believe what they're saying but simply to foment controversy on the air or in print. If a player needed to be media savvy twenty years ago, imagine the pressure today's players have to develop the skills to navigate the modern media minefield!

I understand that sports is a business and that entertainment is big business. But we're losing something. We're losing the personal connection that for decades baseball enjoyed in our society as the preeminent American sport—perhaps in all sports, for that matter. We're losing the sense of appreciation bordering on healthy obsession that riveted children, and even adults, who hungered for information about their teams and their favorite players. When was the last time you met a kid who could keep a box score? When was the last time you met a kid who kept his baseball programs folded neatly away, the most important possessions in his world? Who loved his baseball cards for the players on those cards, and not for the money he could get for them? People don't bring one ball to the ballpark for autographs—it's now a whole bag of balls to be signed for display and sale on eBay.

Society has changed, and sometimes it seems that baseball just doesn't fit in with the way we live our lives today. Critics say the game is too slow, too cerebral, too out of touch with kids who relate more to Xbox than the batter's box, who find more pleasure in viewing extreme sports than watching a savvy batter prolong a pitch count with two outs and men on base.

It's hard enough to keep kids interested in baseball when soaring real estate values means fewer open spaces in urban areas for ball games, and broken city budgets have no money to keep a baseball diamond polished. Cities can't afford to maintain parks and fields. Real estate developers have claimed most of the empty spaces, green fields, and vacant lots in our cities and towns.

Back in the day, parents could let their children wander off on a summer morning to while away the day playing without adult supervision. Today, a legitimate fear of predators keeps parents from letting their children stray from their field of vision. Leave a child unsupervised for six hours and you may be prosecuted or go to jail and the child may be at genuine risk. And with the rise of one-parent and two-job households, who has the time or the energy to teach kids how to play a game, pay the fees to play, travel to practices and games that are no longer in your neighborhood, or even supervise them?

Where are the kids today? Although they're no longer headed in droves to see their local team play, a decent amount (30 percent) went to a major league game in 2005. They're also headed to the places where they can practice their moves on their skateboards. Kids want to master the halfpipe, not the bunt or the suicide squeeze. They don't even throw the ball off a wall by themselves—the best way to improve arm strength, accuracy, fielding, footwork, and so forth. Just as a shooter in basketball incessantly shoots and dribbles to become better, ballplayers use this method to practice on their own. Unstructured play was more prevalent than the practices and games—now it is totally reversed: more games, less practice, and no unstructured or individual play. The end result? Weaker, less accurate arms, players with unsatisfactory baseball instincts and reactions who are more prone to injury and fear of failing, which leads to less overall enjoyment and certainly far less youth participation in the game.

And I can't say I totally blame them. As it is right now, high school girls are a lot more interested in boys who play on the football or basketball teams than in the fellows playing baseball. Who knows? If I had been coming up today, perhaps you might have seen me skating a halfpipe, a debonair six-foot-six Dave Winfield executing 1080s high above the crowds!

I see our younger generation as "at risk"—not just to the dangers of obesity, alcohol, drugs, and crime, but also to losing their connection to the game that has given so much to me and so many others. This is true for all of our nation's young people, and it is especially true for inner-city kids.

In most of our inner cities, there are practically no maintained fields on which to play ball, no money for equipment, and no one to teach the game. Forty years ago, nearly all parents could teach some baseball. This is not the case today. You can't teach it if you've never played it, and many dads today didn't play it and may not love it. The tradition is going away. If baseball is the hardest game to learn, it's also the hardest game to teach and to coach. And if we lose it, it will be a tough job to bring it back.

Today's young African Americans lack not only experience playing baseball but knowledge of what the game has meant historically to our race. Jackie Robinson was the civil rights leader in sports and for our nation. He changed not just professional sports but our society as a whole. One wonders if the hip-hop generation is even aware that the Negro Leagues, with icons Cool Papa Bell, Josh Gibson, and the late, great Buck O'Neil, ever existed, and that baseball, along with boxing, were the dominant sports in our culture? Do young people even know who Jackie Robinson is, or about the abuse, hatred, and credible death threats he received, the sacrifice he made when he crossed baseball's color line sixty years ago?

There's been plenty of talk about Babe Ruth as Barry Bonds caught up with the Babe's home-run record. But there's less talk about Henry Aaron, the true home-run king, who hit 755 home runs. Do young African Americans even know who Aaron is (and that he's still alive and active in baseball), or what he had to face when he sought to break the Babe's record? Do they know what Buck O'Neil meant to the African American community? Do they even recognize his name?

In his new book *Forty Million Dollar Slaves,* author and *New York Times* sportswriter William C. Rhoden tells the chilling story he witnessed of an African American college basketball player wearing a Negro Leagues baseball cap to a practice. The coach commended him on historical sense for wearing the cap. The player said he didn't know anything about the history behind the cap and had never heard of the Negro Leagues. He just bought the cap because it looked cool. The coach explained that there was a time when African Americans were not allowed to compete in Major League Baseball. "Coach," the astonished player replied, "get the f— out of here!"

The economics of the game have changed as well. Major League Baseball can sign fifteen or twenty Latin American prospects for the amount of money it takes to sign even a single first-round high school or college player born in the United States. As a result, the game that Jackie Robinson gave so much of his heart to integrate now has a record low number of African American players—the lowest number since 1970—with that number falling lower and lower every year.

Fans are not always aware of the fact that African Americans only represent 8 percent of major leaguers, down from 28 percent in 1975. This is due in part to the fact that there are so many dark-skinned Latin players in the game today. All of the societal and cultural forces we have discussed so far have also come together to make this a reality. Black kids are far more interested in the NBA and the NFL, sports leagues that have gotten their acts together and that market their games much more effectively than does Major League Baseball. All the glory goes to those high school athletes who can dunk a basketball or catch a football. There's not a lot of attention or full scholarships, let alone glory, for the boys playing baseball.

By contrast, in Latin America, and the Dominican Republic in particular, baseball is the number one game, and has been for a hundred years. Baseball players are the center of their culture, and making it to the major leagues is practically the only ticket out of a life of hardship cutting sugarcane or working at some other form of menial labor. San Pedro de Macorís, a Dominican Republic town of little more than a hundred thousand residents, has produced upward of sixty MLB players of note. No United States city or state can boast those numbers. Major League Baseball has gotten extremely sophisticated with regard to its recruitment of young Latin American ballplayers, but until recently much of American baseball's effort in the Dominican Republic and across Latin America has provided a two-sided coin of great opportunity and great despair, removing the best resources without any regard for the environment left behind.

I'll get more deeply into that later in this book. For now, suffice it to say there's a great hunger among Latin American athletes—especially those in Venezuela, Colombia, Panama, and Cuba—to make it in baseball and in no other sport, and that there's an economic imperative to locate and sign Latin American talent, an imperative for which there is no parallel when it comes to recruiting black athletes in the United States. As a result, the number of African American players—and fans—is in free fall.

An indication of the limited future of the African American in baseball comes from the most recent NCAA College World Series. Less than four percent of the players were African American, and there were no African American head coaches on any of those teams. This is even more significant because players drafted from college have become more preferable to many major league clubs, as they are more mature, experienced, and thought to be closer to becoming major league players, which takes an enormous investment of money and time.

Whenever a problem arises in baseball, the game can't shoot itself in the foot fast enough, trying not to solve the problem but instead covering it up and hoping it will go away. Baseball has lurched from crisis to crisis: a canceled World Series, rough labor relations, a steroids-tainted home-run derby that threatens to demean baseball's most cherished records, confrontations with Pete Rose and his gambling—the list goes on and on. Baseball has been unable—and perhaps unwilling—to develop a better plan to pull itself from the morass of negative issues.

The Players Association, begun by Marvin Miller and currently under the directorship of Don Fehr, is the strongest union in the world and its members are the best paid of any union workers anywhere. This success is a product of much bargaining and a lot of time. When Marvin Miller and Dick Moss came over from the steelworkers' union to create and run the Major League Baseball Players Association in the 1960s, no one knew they would change the course of baseball history. But there has been a cost to its success: the enmity and pitched battles between the owners and the players, the decades of labor strife that finally appear to have ended, and the issue of drug-testing standards, among other problems. While baseball has been going through agonies, other sports have grabbed its fan base and risen to the top of the sports and entertainment pyramid.

Take the NBA. It's not perfect by any stretch, but it seems to solve its problems even before they arise, working out collective bargaining agreements that may not leave everyone completely satisfied but which keep the focus on the game and not on the business of the sport. The NBA has also done something Major League Baseball has not: It has successfully woven itself into modern culture, with its brilliant slogan "I love this game!" and now its "NBA cares!" marketing campaign, featuring A-list celebrities courtside to demonstrate their heartfelt joy at being a part of the NBA.

Both the NBA and the NFL take great pains to market not just the game as a whole but also individual stars, creating a deep sense of connection between players and fans. By contrast, baseball frequently demeans its best players, especially as contract time approaches, for the purpose of knocking a multiyear agreement down by a few million dollars. This shortsighted thinking on baseball's part creates enormous disrespect on the part of the fans for the players, who have been giving their all (at least till they get the big contract!) on their behalf.

The NBA and the NFL are also smart enough to make use of their most beloved former players, as analysts and commentators, and by other means of keeping them in the public eye. By comparison, baseball has no mechanism, aside from the occasional Old Timer's Game at Yankee Stadium, to capitalize on the extremely valuable asset of the fans' connection to their favorite players. Once most players, even the most well-known stars, retire from the game, baseball forgets all about them. The NBA and the NFL are far too smart to do that.

Baseball also neglects its most vital asset: the goodwill and memories created by current and former players. The Hall of Fame is home to only the best one percent of those who played the game. But what about the thousands of living current and former ballplayers who aren't in the hall? Why isn't baseball taking advantage of its ties to this elite group of athletes, who are beloved by generations of fans? There should be a better, more cooperative relationship between players, Major League Baseball, the Negro Leagues institutions, and the National Baseball Hall of Fame.

The NBA and NFL are much savvier about their use of retired players. Major League Baseball spends so much time in crisis management that it devotes only a small amount of its resources to thinking proactively about the use of these players and about how to improve the game. The corporate types relate to the older generation of players, those they watched and identified with while growing up. The players of today are only now amassing their experiences and stories. With former players, there are many legends—today's players are still legends in the making. Baseball's fan base continues to dissipate because of MLB's lack of initiative.

Yes, other sports have their problems and their scandals—baseball is not the only sport to suffer embarrassment due to the on- and off-the-field behavior of its players. At the same time, baseball is the sport least able to cope with its many problems because of the level of distrust between the owners and the players, a troubled relationship that stretches back more than thirty years.

It's hard to believe that anything could be wrong in the world of baseball, given the fact that attendance remains at an all-time high. I can hear you saying, "Dave, what are you so worried about? They're selling tickets! They're selling jerseys! Major League Baseball and the players resolved collective bargaining without a hitch last fall. We're reaching out internationally. It's all good!"

But let me ask you this: How many baseball players are heroes to your kid? How many guys are worthy of your support and encouragement today? Perhaps you can name them locally, but few capture national attention or acclaim. In years past, there were more players you looked up to. You might not have known all the facts about their private lives, but they took seriously their responsibility as role models.

They were heroes.

Kids wanted to be like Willie Mays and Harmon Killebrew. Now they only want to be like Mike, Magic, Kobe, or LeBron—

on and off the court. Today, the average baseball fan can barely name more than half a dozen players from his own city's team, because the players move around so much. Is baseball in dire straits? Of course not. It's making tons of money. Attendance records continue to be broken. Many fans have forgiven the game for strikes, scandals, and steroids. Here's my point:

It's good, but it's not *all* good.

It could be so much better.

Right now, baseball's credibility as a sport is eroding so rapidly that the comparisons to World Wrestling Entertainment may not be far away. Baseball's labor troubles leave the game a notch above the NHL in terms of a guarantee that games will be played and seasons will not be lost. Other sports—even extreme sports, NASCAR, and golf—are developing fans by the legions and eating increasingly larger shares of that sports entertainment pie and the "mind share" of fans, in ways baseball can only envy.

My purpose in writing this book is to offer a plan for restoring baseball to its proper place in the minds of Americans, to put the luster back in the game and the game back in the lives of our kids. I don't intend to just rail about what is bad, but to offer suggestions for how things could be different. I know some people might say, "Dave is just upset because he didn't make the kind of money players make today!" Don't fool yourselves. I did all right. The reality is that I made a good deal of money, and continue to lead a very good, fulfilling life.

My reason for communicating with you and with everyone else who loves the game is that I just can't accept having baseball fall into sports oblivion, with little respect and passionless participation. I can see the trend heading downward—not just among African American players and fans but also among too many Americans in general.

You can say that we've all dropped the ball—the commissioner's office, the owners, the Players Association, local government, parks and recreation departments, and even parents and fans. If baseball is to recover from its series of self-inflicted wounds, if the game is to regain its place as America's pastime, and if the game is to appeal to this and future generations of young people, especially those in our urban areas, we all have to get busy. Baseball is not unaware of the challenges and problems it faces, from its image problems, to its inability to attract more African American players and fans, to its falling ratings in the surveys that ask Americans which sport they love the most.

Yet the responses on the part of baseball—the commissioner, the owners, and the players—have usually been piecemeal, addressing a single issue for a period of time, but never focusing on the big picture. Not in partnership, not long-term, not from the heart and head together. I believe the collective-bargaining bickering and animus have subsided and there will be civil relations, but have we arrived at a true working relationship yet? No.

Indeed, the game I love is hurting. The pace of baseball is slow and leisurely, seemingly out of step with our warp-speed lives. Other sports are faster, often louder, and frequently much more dangerous than baseball. Many require little coaching and you are free to improvise and learn on your own. You can do that in baseball, but the locations and environments to do so are disappearing rapidly. World Series games begin so late and often end past midnight, robbing generations of potential new fans the opportunity to see great endings to great games. Could you imagine that for the Super Bowl? The simple reason: TV money dictates schedules.

As we are losing our younger fans, baseball is hemorrhaging fans of African American descent. The Latin American and Spanish-speaking contingent is being addressed by advertising and local marketing initiatives, as those fan bases continue to grow. While baseball does have some solid programs to promote the game in urban communities, these programs are not connected to one another. I don't see urban music stars or African

American cultural or political icons promoting baseball, though I do know they attend and enjoy the game. Let's involve these important people! There is no *organized campaign* to preserve baseball's legacy and to keep the flame alive, and there needs to be such a campaign.

To its credit, last year Major League Baseball opened its first Urban Academy and baseball educational center in Compton, an inner-city community in Los Angeles. When did they start talking about creating the Urban Academy? All the way back in 1999! Unfortunately it took seven years to build a ten-million-dollar facility, a few ball fields, locker rooms, and training areas, and a program to train inner-city prospects, and give them education, motivation, and guidance regarding baseball-related careers. It is imperative that the Major League Baseball Urban Youth Academy program succeeds, because other subsequent Urban Academies in key major markets are contingent upon Los Angeles's leadership and success.

I want to see an ongoing, comprehensive, multiyear campaign—you might call it "Baseball United"—that brings together the commissioner, the Players Association, MLB alumni, the owners, the fans, corporate America, concerned and dedicated citizens, the media, and, most important, our youngest generation of kids, to ensure the game's future and its importance for all Americans.

Playing baseball remains one of the hardest physical tasks that any human being can do. It's been said over and over that hitting a baseball is the single hardest skill to learn in organized sports. Basketball and football players can jump from college right to the professional level and contribute, enjoying the glamour of the draft and the accompanying money.

But baseball remains the epitome of delayed gratification. Few high school players have ever successfully jumped to the major leagues and managed to stick. Even college players from solid programs often have to spend years in the minor leagues, perfecting their ability to hit the curveball or hit the cutoff man. The required repetition and mental toughness of playing at the MLB level is formidable. In an era of instant gratification, young players just don't have the time to learn the skills to play the game correctly, and now, many of today's prospective fans don't take the time to understand or appreciate the nuances of the game.

I will oftentimes debate with friends, comparing and contrasting a Major League Baseball career with the career of a successful athlete in the NFL or the NBA. By the end of the conversation, most of these friends—which include parents and children of all ages—exclaim, "I didn't know that!" in reference to a piece of information I gave them about baseball. Most of my friends leave such conversations with changed opinions, now favoring baseball as their hypothetical sport of choice, careerwise.

Baseball. Is it too old, too slow, too boring for today's fast-paced world?

I say no way. I say baseball is just as exciting, challenging, beautiful, thrilling, and satisfying as any sport you can find on TV or in a stadium. For generations, baseball was *the* national pastime, with perhaps only boxing at times rivaling it for the nation's attention. Decades ago, you couldn't give away tickets to NBA games. When Bill Russell was the man in the NBA, you could walk up to the box office window at Boston Garden or anywhere else in the country and buy a ticket to see him play. Sold-out arenas were rare. We also tend to forget that the first two Super Bowls didn't even sell out.

At the same time, the reality is that during the last four decades, sports has become a big business in the United States. It's no longer just about playing games. There's big money to be made on every aspect of the game, from tickets, concessions, television, performances, sports marketing, athlete representation, and so on. Players today more often than not consider themselves performers, entertainers, and businessmen, and not just athletes. They ask, "What kind of money can my performance or on-field and off-field antics generate?" The sense of entitlement and "get rich" expectations changed the relationship between athletes and fans. Money has all but stripped away the innocence of sports. It's neither good nor bad; it is simply a fact of modern sports, be it amateur or professional.

Those who love the game must ask themselves, Who's minding the store? Disparities between wealthy and poor teams seem to increase with each passing year. Until recently, the owners cried poverty yet spent dizzying amounts on salaries. The fans had no interest in trying to understand their plight. Often teams pay for ballplayers who are has-beens, or those who never even had it in the first place. Today, players do well, despite their ability or tenure. Decades of labor strife has left fans angry and confused. When it comes to issues that affect the integrity of the game, like steroids and other performance-enhancing drugs, people will always remember that no one seemed to be leading the charge to eradicate illegal performance-enhancing drugs. Both sides were forced to make changes by Congress and negative media attention. The saga of one of baseball's greatest players, Barry Bonds, will get worse before it gets better. According to a recent survey, half of all baseball fans hope that Bonds will fail to break Aaron's home-run record because they believe he cheated.

We have yet to hit the nadir. In the Bible, the Book of Proverbs tells us, "Where there is no vision, the people perish"—that's another reason I decided to write this book. I hope I will open some eyes and incite passionate action to bring about change.

Let me make it clear that I'm not using this platform to call out individuals, or to rant and rave the way they do on sports talk shows. Instead, my intention is to bring about awareness to baseball fans, and to make an impassioned plea to everyone who loves the game of baseball to recognize that the game we love is being hollowed out. A lot of people are coming to think that the great American pastime is past its time. I strongly disagree, but we all need to take some radical steps to salvage it.

I'll use the term *Baseball United* throughout this book as a name for my plan for baseball's recovery, although you can call it whatever you want, as long as everyone with an interest and/or ability to do something about it comes on board. At the end of each chapter, I'll offer specific suggestions for the individuals and entities discussed in that chapter, so that they have some clear directives for how to take part in baseball's resurgence.

We've all heard the talk of problems, but I don't hear anyone saying nearly enough about what might be done to improve the situation. I want to do more than illuminate the issues. I want to show you what actions you can take, whatever group you represent or wherever you are in the game—as long as you care about baseball. I invite you to join me on a journey that will touch on baseball's history, on matters of race and economics, and on the pure pleasure that comes from watching a great pitch, a beautiful play in the field, or a commanding home run, or even just experiencing a safe, affordable, and enjoyable time with your family at the ballpark.

Baseball has never had a comprehensive plan to address all of the issues it faces. Now it does. So let's see if we can pick up the ball and make the play!

CHAPTER 1

Major League Baseball

I am constantly asking my friends inside Major League Baseball and the Players Association the same question little kids ask their parents during a long car trip: "Are we there yet?" Have we reached an amicable working relationship between those on the field and those in the front office? So far, the best answer I've received is, "It has definitely improved, but we are still not there yet."

If the game of baseball is to regain its position as the national pastime, if Baseball United is ever to get off the ground, the impetus for change has to come from the commissioner and Major League Baseball. That's because most of the power and money to fuel such change reside with the commissioner's office. But it has to be accomplished through a partnership, and the commissioner's partner has to be the Major League Baseball Players Association and the individual players. Neither side can do it alone. While I hope that every team, every player, every youth baseball coach, every fan, every town and city, and every media resource and corporation will ultimately become involved in the initiative, baseball is simply too big an entity to be transformed from the ground up.

Some changes may take place at the grassroots level, but if baseball is serious about ensuring its future, then direction, motivation, and leadership have to come from the top. And when it comes to Major League Baseball, the buck stops with the commissioner.

The most important thing that the baseball commissioner can do is to restore a sense of trust between owners and players. Baseball's labor history over the past forty years has been anything but smooth. Until Curt Flood challenged the reserve clause in the late 1960s, baseball teams essentially owned a player for the life of his major league career. In legal terms, the relationship of a team owner to an individual player in those days could have been described as adhesion: One side (the owners) had virtually all the bargaining power, while the other side (the players) was stuck with whatever the owners might offer. It's important to remember that the Curt Flood case created the schism between players and owners. However, it's naïve to assume that labor and management have only been at odds for the past twenty years. It goes back much further than that.

Baseball history is replete with accounts of players who came off championship years only to find themselves confronted with take-it-or-leave-it contracts that offered a minimum raise, no raise at all, or even a *reduction* in salary from the previous year. Until thirty years ago, there was no such thing as a player's agent. Before the 1970s, a player "negotiated" his contract by appearing at the office of the wealthy, imperious team owner, who handed him a pen and a contract with a number typed in. The player's options were to sign the contract or to risk demotion, either to the minor leagues or to some awful competing team. In other words, players had no leverage at all.

In 1966, Los Angeles Dodgers pitchers Don Drysdale and Sandy Koufax made baseball history with a joint holdout that led to salary breakthroughs for both of them. But even these two pitchers, commonly ranked among baseball's best ever, could not be certain that their holdout would lead to any financial benefits at all. They had no idea whether the Dodgers would give them more money, or inform them that their services were no longer required. Since their contracts contained the reserve clause, which bound players to teams for life, Koufax and Drysdale could not have put in their time and waited to become free agents. The concept of free agency was still a decade away. The legal term *adhesion* comes from the same root from which we derive the word *adhesive,* and it has exactly the same meaning. Even two of the greatest pitchers of their era—or any era—were stuck.

Things changed when Curt Flood told the St. Louis Cardinals that he would not accept a trade to Philadelphia. His refusal to report to the Phillies set in motion a chain of events that eventually led to the United States Supreme Court ruling on his case. It took four long years from the moment when Flood first vetoed the trade until his right—and the rights of all baseball players—to refuse trades and have a say in his career were granted. In that time, Flood's baseball career suffered enormously. He was the target of vituperative hate mail and was looked upon as a renegade by the media and by fans. Nonetheless, Flood was a groundbreaker, paving the way for all baseball players—and perhaps even all professional athletes—to economic freedom.

A few years before Flood's case began to wend its way slowly through the courts, a new figure emerged on the baseball labor relations scene. In 1966, Marvin Miller, a former negotiator for the steel workers' union, became the leader of the newly formed Major League Players Association, and took his message of players' rights from team to team during the 1968 spring training. Though soft-spoken, Miller was articulate and effective in organizing and galvanizing this group of men to speak up and ask for their rights. In fact, Miller was tough, feisty, and, to the owners' way of thinking, a cancer on the game of baseball. Players quickly came around to Miller's way of thinking: that they were entitled to the same kind of economic rights for which he had fought so hard for his steelworkers.

Miller's leadership and strength were formidable, and he challenged baseball's prevailing ethos, which gave all of the power and rights to the owners. By the time he stepped down in 1983 (much to the relief of the owners, no doubt), baseball players enjoyed unprecedented freedom and were making record amounts of money. I was there through every bit of it—the smoke-filled collective-bargaining sessions, with both sides displaying frayed nerves and not-so-subtle contempt for each other. In a matter of years, the power had shifted.

That shift did not come without a cost, however. From 1972 until 1995, baseball endured no fewer than eight strikes or lockouts, the last of which wiped away the last few months of 1995 and that year's World Series. Few people remember that Ken Griffey Jr. had been on a tear that season to break Roger Maris's then-prevailing single-season home-run record (and without the aid of andro or other performance-enhancing substances, legal or otherwise). As Griffey ruefully remarked, "I picked a bad year to have a good year."

Baseball's labor strife hurt more than Griffey—it hurt the game itself. Fans, who had watched with increasing wariness as the major league players' agreement expired every three or four years, deserted the game in droves after the debacle of a canceled postseason, returning to the game only in 1998, when a friendly rivalry between Mark McGwire and Sammy Sosa over who would break Maris's record first drew interest back to baseball. A dozen years after that canceled World Series, baseball's popularity has returned, due in no small part to the Sosa–McGwire home-run derby and the many new beautiful, family-friendly ballparks that have sprung up around the country.

Other innovations have increased the game's popularity, most notably the multitiered playoff system. It might be anathema to baseball purists, but having three divisions and a wild-card winner in each league means that more teams—and thus more fans—remain involved in pennant races, often right down to the last week of the season. Baseball playoffs are well attended and capture the attention of a large national viewing audience. The reduction in the length of games, the introduction of the World Baseball Classic, new ballparks, and extraordinary TV contracts have renewed public interest in baseball. So the game is definitely doing a lot of things right, despite its repeated missteps year after year after year.

That brings us to the present day. The memories of almost forty years of labor unrest, strikes, collusion, lockouts, and congressional drug hearings—all of which received extensive media coverage—have left the game with a bitter legacy of mistrust between the owners on one side, the Players Association on the other, and the office of the commissioner in the middle.

Yes, it's vital for the commissioner to be up-front on the many issues that confront the game today, most notably illegal drugs, the marketing of baseball around the world, and other pressing issues. But the most important thing the commissioner can do is establish a level of trust that leads to a true working relationship between the owners and the players. There is absolutely nothing more important for the future of the game. To paraphrase Abraham Lincoln, "A house divided cannot stand." Although both camps are strong, I say unequivocally, *the game cannot be all it can be until both sides work together*—in joint marketing, joint advertising, and joint business ventures. An industry with such a volatile labor-management relationship will have a very difficult time competing with other sports entertainment industries, and that is exactly the fate that has befallen baseball over the last few decades. As I write, the players and owners have taken the first step toward concluding collective bargaining before the deadline, and have done so without launching public volleys at each other.

It's no coincidence that as labor unrest and mistrust between owners and players has risen, fan interest in the game has diminished. From my behind-the-scenes discussions with executives in both camps, things have gotten better, but they are far from where they need to be. There's no other major sport where owners and players find themselves at loggerheads so much of the time, with such a deep reservoir of mistrust between them. (The only possible exception is hockey, a sad comparison, indeed, given the severity of that sport's problems.) Think about it: The NFL and the NBA, for all their imperfections, have a remarkable record of labor peace. And when was the last time you ever heard of the PGA locking out Tiger Woods from the U.S. Open?

It rarely happens in those other sports, and yet it happens in baseball, year after year. It's easy to say that the game is doing fine—records are being set every day, and not just on the playing field. Every year, teams reach new records in terms of their over-all value, with some teams and ancillary businesses topping the billion-dollar mark. Television revenue continues to set new records. Advertising and sponsorship revenues are soaring over $5 billion, and growing. Success often breeds complacency, a sense that if it isn't broke, why fix it?

And yet, for years the overwhelming majority of Major League Baseball teams have been crying that they are losing money. They haven't opened their books to the public, so fans have no way of verifying their claims of destitution and corporate poverty. But if the teams really are that broke, wouldn't it make sense for somebody to step in and try to fix something?

I hope that the commissioner's office will embrace the Base-ball United campaign this book advocates for Major League Baseball. Without cooperative support from MLB management and the players, the campaign is doomed to failure, no matter how many enlightened, forward-thinking individuals line up behind it. Support for any major shift in the way baseball thinks about itself, markets itself, and looks to its own future can only succeed if those who hold the reins want it to succeed.

Therefore, without the commissioner solidly behind a cam-paign for change in MLB, nothing will happen. The media would see the whole initiative as little more than baseless wishful thinking, or smoke and mirrors—the fond hope of one retired

Hall of Famer. So maximum support from the commissioner's office is the fundamental prerequisite for this plan to catch fire and make a difference. And yet, what will happen if the commissioner attempts to launch Baseball United without the full support and commitment, involvement, and, above all, trust of the players? It won't work.

Without the full support of the Players Association and the players themselves, the campaign would still be doomed to failure. Unless the commissioner's office first works to regain the trust of the players and establishes a mutually beneficial, cooperative platform, it's unthinkable that the players would embrace a plan they might well see as a force-fed public relations move.

We live in an era where everyone is incredibly media savvy, from the youngest fan to the most veteran member of the sports media, from the players in the dugout to the owners in their luxury boxes. They know what's real and they know what's a publicity stunt. There's no fooling anyone in today's information-saturated environment. Unless the commissioner can truly enlist the cooperation of the Players Association and the players themselves, there's no future for any of the plans I mention in this book. And there's no possibility of the baseball establishment taking a program from the commissioner's office seriously unless the fundamental issue of trust between MLB owners and the players is addressed. There has to be a bridge and a solid platform upon which to work.

I'm not talking about reestablishing a bond that became tarnished over time. I'm talking about creating something that has never existed in modern baseball. The commissioner is charged with representing the best interests of baseball, and yet historically the commissioner and his office have stood up more readily for the best interests of the owners than those of the players.

We're talking about a major paradigm shift, not a return to imaginary halcyon days when everybody in the baseball industry got along just fine. Let's not tell lies—they never did get along just fine. Not now, not when I was playing, and not fifty years before that, when Judge Kenesaw Mountain Landis was banishing members of the "Black Sox" for their role in throwing the 1919 World Series. Before 1947, blacks were not allowed to play, and Latinos had to have light skin to slip in. The owners and the players have never "gotten along." This does not mean, however, that they cannot recognize their common interest in a future where everyone thrives and wins, and forge a new path together in this new century.

In late October 2006, we saw that both sides recognized what was at stake, and resolved their monetary issues even before the deadline without issuing negative commentary. Progress is indeed being made. Now that they are married, how will the honeymoon and living arrangements work out?

Baseball simply has too much to lose. The experience of the NHL's lost 2004–2005 season ought to be a cautionary tale to both sides. Stubbornness, egotism, and perhaps even downright foolishness on the part of hockey's owners and players resulted in the loss of an entire season, hundreds of millions of dollars of revenue, and a considerable part of the fan base that may never be coaxed back to the game. That's sports management shortsightedness at its worst. As I was writing this chapter it was not unthinkable, given the current level of mistrust between players and owners, that instead of a new collective-bargaining agreement, we might have ended up with a collective suicide pact that knocks the game down so hard, it can't get up. You could have argued that baseball has too much at stake to let something like that happen, but you could have made the same argument about hockey in the weeks before its lost season finally slipped away. As the limbo singers used to ask, "How low can you go?"

I hope that baseball never has to discover the answer to that question. I have a great deal of personal regard for Bud Selig, the commissioner of Major League Baseball, and I wouldn't want anything in this book to detract from my respect for him or from the respect I have for the Players Association's Don Fehr, for that matter. The problem is that Commissioner Selig operates in a media environment that thrives on scandal and disunity. There is a sense of endless crisis befalling the game today, whether the headlines involve yet another ballplayer suspended for steroid use or any of the other ills that plague the game. On this front, Commissioner Selig will have to be proactive with Don Fehr to build that bridge to higher ground.

I think the commissioner does an admirable job of handling the steady flow of crises with which he is forced to deal. And yet, there's more to dealing with the media than simply fending off crisis after crisis. When I was playing for the Yankees and living in the harsh glare of the attention of the New York media, I learned that dealing with the media is a lot like boxing. There was offense, defense, and there was counterpunching. The defensive side of dealing with the media has to do with handling what comes at you, coping with allegations and scandals as best you can while recognizing that the public is sick and tired of downbeat news, despite the media's endless appetite for stories that cast the game in a negative light. Baseball needs to take the offensive, not just fend off those blows and get in the occasional counterpunch at the media. To my mind, taking the offense with the media means presenting a new leadership approach—what I'm talking about with regard to Baseball United.

In a perfect world, the commissioner's office, with the assistance and support of the Players Association, would use the Baseball United program as a fulcrum for shaping media and fan perceptions of the sport and for changing the way baseball addresses its in-house business. You can't sell the media hype, and you can't get them to run public relations stories as news. And yet, there are so many ways that Baseball United can generate hard news that casts baseball in a positive light. The best interests of baseball require us not only to defend and counterpunch, but to take the offensive in the war for the public's attention.

It wasn't too many years ago that stock car racing was ridiculed as the proprietary interest of beer-guzzling good ol' boys in remote pockets of the South. Now, NASCAR routinely fills its tracks with crowds of one hundred fifty thousand or more. In early 2006, a televised *rainout* of a NASCAR race outdrew a nationally televised, late-season NBA contest between the Los Angeles Lakers and the Cleveland Cavaliers, featuring the marquee matchup of Kobe Bryant versus LeBron James. A rainout—those cars weren't even moving around the track! And yet more people tuned in to watch the rain fall on Talladega than to watch Kobe and LeBron work their magic on the court.

Take a guess what the fastest-growing sport in America is today. It's not what you think. It's not baseball, that's for sure. It's not even football or basketball or auto racing.

It's bull riding.

Think I'm joking? I'm not. Bull riding, although small in comparison, packs arenas from Las Vegas to Madison Square Garden. Corporate sponsorship is going through the roof. So is TV exposure. Bull riding, according to the *Los Angeles Times,* is the fastest-growing sport in America. And that's no bull!

The point of all this is that in the world of sports, as in every other aspect of life, nothing remains stagnant. A few generations ago, baseball was the king of sports. Even the powerful NBA, which rose to preeminence with stars like Magic Johnson, Michael Jordan, and Larry Bird, finds itself taking a backseat to stock car racing. That's why I am trying to make the point that even though the game of baseball today is successful, the base of its success is hollowed out and getting smaller every year, while more media-savvy sports and entertainment events are leaching fans' mind share—and revenue—away from the once-proud national pastime.

Twenty years ago, President Ronald Reagan stood before the Berlin Wall and issued a challenge to the leader of the Soviet Union. "President Gorbachev," he famously said, "tear down that wall!" Commissioner Selig, I urge you and Don Fehr to do nothing less. The future of the game depends on it, and it just makes good business sense.

As we discussed in the prologue, some of the key issues facing baseball have to do with race and economics. If the commissioner's office is truly in charge of the game of baseball, then surely the commissioner must recognize the fact that the number of African American ballplayers is continuing to diminish. There are several reasons for this decline, some of which (i.e., diversity in business relationships and human resources) the commissioner has the power to do something about.

With regard to players in Major League Baseball, Commissioner Selig can do something about the disparity of opportunities among three groups of prospects: inner-city African Americans, Latin American ballplayers, and white American kids from comfortable backgrounds. The top one hundred Latin ballplayers last year earned more than half a billion dollars in salary, a large portion of which goes back into the communities. I begrudge no one his success, but what does that mean for inner-city communities in the United States—the very places that used to be hotbeds for fresh talent? Organized baseball is spending millions and millions of dollars developing talent in Latin America, Japan, and even Australia. But how much is organized baseball really doing back home, and is organized baseball providing enough support for adequate baseball fields, equipment, and coaching for the next generation of urban and/or African American players?

A simple look around any inner-city neighborhood would tell you that the answer is no. Surely there is much more that the commissioner's office could be doing to ensure that young people, even those from economically deprived backgrounds, have an equal opportunity to fall in love with the game of baseball, and learn what it takes to compete in the game at the highest levels.

In addition, even though they perform better than the NFL and

NBA, the commissioner's office and MLB could use more diversity in their management ranks—not just of color, but also of age and gender, so as to be more in touch with the game and its fans. Input from youth at this juncture is critical. The key advisors and decision makers tend to be attorneys and older individuals, mostly from the same socioeconomic stratum who are not as in tune with youth culture, music, and entertainment.

Another thought: Why not have special made-for-TV events, like the ESPYs or the Heisman Trophy award ceremony, for baseball's most important honors and events—the June draft, and the Cy Young, Rookie of the Year, and Most Valuable Player awards? This would be a great way to have the focus remain on baseball even after the season has ended. The ESPYs now have a golf tournament, special banquets, and a multitude of other made-for-media events. What does baseball do to announce its MVPs and Cy Young winners? It just sends out a press release. Where's the red carpet? Where are the klieg lights? Where are the players? More important, where are the fans? All of these elements remain on the sidelines until there is a better working relationship.

I have no illusions that the commissioner of baseball and the head of the Players Association will suddenly embrace Baseball United or each other. I was even approached by a colleague who expressed concern that I would be attacked in the media or marginalized for voicing my ideas. I'm not afraid of that. If not me, who? If not now, when?

Revenue sharing is working but the players want MLB teams to ensure they will spend some of the money and not just take profits without investing in the team. In his recent book *In the Best Interests of Baseball? The Revolutionary Reign of Bud Selig,* sports economist Andrew Zimbalist points out that practically everything the commissioner of baseball does comes back to affect the players in some way. Take the issue of revenue sharing. Under this practice, large-market teams agree to bestow some financial largesse on their less well-to-do brethren. The idea is to ensure, or at least create the possibility for, competitive balance. You can only go so far in terms of keeping your allegiance of fans if some market teams are all but shut out of the postseason for decades at a time, and that's certainly been the case. From a player's point of view, what could be wrong with revenue sharing, since it theoretically permits all teams—and therefore all players—a shot at World Series glory?

The answer is subtle but powerful. Zimbalist gives the example of a player who might be worth $20 million to a team over the course of a season. That's because more people would buy season tickets, individual tickets, jerseys, beer, programs, parking, you name it—and it adds up to $20 million in revenue for the team. The economic value of that player to his team becomes a key factor in determining just how much the team can offer him in salary. It works out, on average, that teams pay their players approximately 50 percent of the revenue they generate. So an individual who earns a team $20 million will likely end up with a salary of approximately $10 million.

You don't have to have a good year on the field to have a good year at the bank. Don Fehr was quoted in an AP story that posted on Yahoo! Sports on February 9, 2006, as saying, "There are teams in Major League Baseball that receive more money from central baseball from the national television contract and revenue sharing than they spend on payrolls." That's before they sell a ticket, or a hot dog, or a beer, or a parking space. We have to be concerned about the incentives of this system.

A team that makes $20 million in revenue because it has a particular star player is now obliged to share some of its wealth with other teams, including those that cannot or will not pay more money to put stars in their lineups. Let's say that the team that did hire that superstar ends up with $20 million worth of revenue, just as expected. Under revenue sharing, that team will now have to take $10 million and ship it off to a small-market team. Well, if a player can bring in $20 million but half of that will be transferred to another franchise, then the real economic value of the player to his team is just $10 million, the amount left after revenue sharing is deducted. If the team is only going to pay about half of his value as salary, how much would the team be willing to pay him? Five million dollars.

So even the decision to institute revenue sharing ends up hurting the players. If a player is worth less to a franchise because of revenue sharing, count on the fact that the team is going to offer him less in salary.

Makes me glad they didn't have revenue sharing when I was playing!

Despite this imperfection, I believe revenue sharing is a positive step toward creating competitive balance. It could only have taken place under a commissioner like Bud Selig, who has the ear of all thirty team owners because of his generally likable nature, his consensus-building capabilities, and his desire to work with the teams to make baseball succeed.

Zimbalist also points out that the commissioner's office was created as a reaction to the infamous Black Sox scandal of 1919, in which players on the Chicago White Sox threw the World Series in order to receive payment from gamblers. The integrity of the game was on the line, so the owners acted to create a commissioner who could restore confidence in the game. For decades, thanks to baseball's antitrust exemption and limited competition from other sports, baseball was pretty much the only game in town.

It wasn't until 1958 that pro football first became a factor in American society. The NBA really didn't take off until the eighties, with the advent of the rivalry between Magic Johnson and Larry Bird, the ascendancy of one Michael Jordan, and the marketing genius of NBA commissioner David Stern. Since baseball had the American appetite for sports all but locked up for the first sixty years of the twentieth century, the commissioner of baseball did not need to think like a businessman. He simply needed to be the symbol of integrity, the guarantor of public trust in the game. He did not need to represent the players at all. He was simply responsible for making sure that fans thought the game was on the level.

The key dilemma presented by the commissioner's office is that the position was created by the owners to serve "the best interests of baseball"—but only as defined by the owners. Neither the players nor the fans had any say in the selection of the commissioner, and the commissioner could be fired by the owners at any time if he incurred their wrath. He was always the owners' man, plain and simple.

So Commissioner Selig inherited this heralded position laden with the distrust of the players, since many commissioners of baseball in fact saw themselves as the representative of the owners and were often outspoken about this perceived role.

Many times in the last twenty years, events have made the relationship between the players and the owners/commissioner contentious and acrimonious. These challenges have included baseball's experience with collusion in the 1980s, when the teams essentially agreed not to offer large salaries to the best players available on the free-agent market. The attempted imposition of a drug-testing policy without the consent of the Players Association was another such flash point.

Improving the relationship between owners and players will be no small task. But if anyone can do it, Bud Selig and Don Fehr can. They both recognize that the interests of baseball are not served when its major constituencies are deeply at odds. They both recognize the importance of the "league think" attitude—the idea of putting the league's interests ahead of individual interests—that the NFL mastered under Commissioners Burt Bell, Pete Rozelle, and Paul Tagliabue. Baseball has made its joint financial contributions to the 9/11 fund, and to a degree to the Katrina disaster. Their most successful partnership was the World Baseball Classic in 2006.

It's time for the historic animosity between baseball's labor and management to end. This requires more than just labor peace. It's time to view baseball as a unique entity in which cooperation rather than competition or collusion is the rule. It's time to establish a commitment toward an issue that brings baseball back to the fans and once again captures their love and respect—this is what I am talking about. And a transformation like this has to come from the top.

CHAPTER 2

The Owners

They call them the "Lords of Baseball" because they answer to almost no one but themselves. Much has been written in recent years about baseball owners' attempts to milk the maximum amount of revenues while crying abject poverty at the same time. Is it fair for a team like the Tampa Bay Devil Rays or the Pittsburgh Pirates to minimize its payroll, putting a barely major league–level team on the field while charging major league prices for tickets, concessions, and parking, and still collect luxury-tax money from wealthier teams? For a long time, the ownership of the Minnesota Twins, my home team growing up, was notorious for paying its ballplayers as little as possible. Should teams today be permitted to put a second-rate team on the field so as to maximize revenues? What should the owners be required to do in order to remain competitive, and in order to keep the faith of their teams' fan bases?

At the opposite extreme is George Steinbrenner, who commonly "sets the market" for free agents, and for signing players at all levels, by lavishing cash on the ballplayers he covets. The Yankees are still number one in overall team payroll. Is "Steinbrenner money" creating disparities between the haves and have-nots? How far can a small-market team really go when it has to compete against free-spending teams like the Yankees, Red Sox, and other pennant-winning teams of the last decade?

Then there is the question of who is watching those players perform. Major League Baseball has documented a steady and severe decline in the number of African American spectators. And yet, baseball has done almost nothing about it to this point. The sport appears to be kissing off an entire generation of black fans, leaving a lot of money on the table and disaffecting the parents of some potentially great players of the future. People question the attitude of baseball's owners and the commissioner's office, an attitude that seems to be, "Why bother marketing to African Americans? We've got plenty of other fans."

Even as I write, there actually is movement and action—it's just been slow in coming, and it hasn't been inclusive or comprehensive. This is unacceptable. In my role as vice president and senior advisor of the San Diego Padres, I have introduced a marketing plan to promote baseball to the urban and African American communities, and to increase baseball's connections to the minority business community, with concessions participation and employment. *We are nowhere close to where we want to be or should be.* I can see that people are afraid to break out of their comfort zone, but they need to. Every team should be taking similar steps. Otherwise, we will lose a generation of urban and African American parents and children.

Because of my experiences in Major League Baseball, I can give a view of the top from both camps—the owners and the Players Association. There are risks attached to being a Major League Baseball team owner anywhere outside of New York, Boston, or Chicago. Think about it: A team owner is a business person who works his entire life to build a fortune, in the process becoming a legend in his industry, if not a household name. After leaping all the hurdles to get to this position, he now finds himself blamed for everything from the high cost of player salaries to steroids, not to mention the cost of a beer at the stadium.

In some ways, he can do no right. If he fails to sign expensive free agents, either because he does not believe they are worth the salaries they command or because he has a strategy of utilizing homegrown talent, he is vilified by the local media and the fans for being a tightwad. If, on the other hand, he spends a small fortune on the salary of a few free agents who fail to perform at Hall of Fame levels, he gets criticized yet again, this time for selecting poorly. Even if his picks do perform well, he still comes under the microscope because he has to raise the price of tickets, food, and drink at the ballpark in order to pay for those big free-agent salaries.

He is truly damned if he does and damned if he doesn't.

He comes under intense suspicion from fellow team owners for every move he makes. If he is spending a lot of money on free agents, the other owners criticize him for "failing to hold the line," a line they themselves hold only when it is convenient for them. When he does not spend much money on his team, his fellow owners accuse him of pocketing revenue-sharing money instead of using it for its true purpose, to help create competitive balance on the field.

It's not as though all baseball owners rush to embrace the new guys. In point of fact, owners are far more divided than many fans realize, along big-market/small-market lines and with regard to other philosophical and business differences. For the commissioner of baseball, riding herd on these unruly millionaires and billionaires is a lot like herding cats.

At the same time, the owners cannot be said to have played their roles as guardians of the game in a perfect manner. Who can forget collusion, when, in the mid-1980s, the owners decided unilaterally not to hire any free agents, so as to eliminate the bargaining power of the players? The strategy backfired and caused deep, festering wounds. The Players Association certainly can't forget that episode no matter who's in charge of the union.

Once you get away from Boston and the two New York teams,

the rest of the league operates on a relatively tight budget. The Padres this year, for example, have to compete on a budget of $70+ million for player payroll and now a mortgage on a great new ballpark. They simply can't afford to wave the checkbook, Steinbrenner-style, at every free agent who comes along (as much as we would like to). There are also imposed guidelines from Major League Baseball regarding EBITDA (Earnings Before Interest, Tax and Debt Amortization) and debt reduction that teams are governed by as well. Of course, the fans love Steinbrenner and there are more New York Yankee fans than for any other ball club in Major League Baseball, but the rest of the country would like to see a more level playing field, where more teams can compete for the championship each year. This policy seems to be working, as the range of teams that have won the World Series in the past years is wider. Baseball can now claim the playing field is more level than in other major sports.

The owners also receive a great deal of criticism and blame for the fact that baseball lacked a comprehensive drug policy for so many years. Many believe that the owners should have known what was going on in their clubhouses—which players were getting big and strong practically overnight, which players had "personal trainers" of questionable morality, and so on. The reasoning is that since the owners viewed their best players as the financial foundation of their franchises, they were not about to question the inflated performances of their players. Therefore, the question that remains is whether baseball owners were willing to violate the integrity of the game in exchange for the possibility of one or more winning seasons.

I don't think it's entirely fair to single out the owners for the fact that baseball lacked a comprehensive drug policy for so many years. Even if all the owners had wanted such a program, the players' union remained adamantly against it, claiming that the mere existence of a drug-testing program was an unconstitutional violation of privacy and also a presumption of guilt on their part.

It's hard to know which owners would have demanded a drug-treatment policy if the Players Association had been more open to one, and it's hard to know which owners might not have cared.

I think everyone in Major League Baseball, owners and players alike, wishes they could have the last ten years back, with regard to the effects of steroids, HGH, and amphetamines on the game. Hindsight is always twenty-twenty. If the owners knew then what we know now, they would have been much more aggressive about policing even their superstars. If they knew what was being done in the dark, they would have forbidden the proliferation of drug culture in the sport. It's not just the integrity of the game, that all-important intangible, that has been sullied as a result of the drug mess. The bodies of the superstars themselves, and the bodies of many a marginal player, were pretty much destroyed by the very drugs that gave them a real or perceived power boost.

I haven't read Jose Canseco's book *Juiced* because I honestly just don't want to, but I understand that he says something to the effect that drugs are here to stay and that they will actually enhance the quality of the game for players and fans. I just laughed when I heard that. I don't see that at all. There's always a bell curve of players—some who will take drugs no matter what, some who won't no matter what, and the broad swath of players in the middle who aren't quite sure what's best for them, their bodies, or their careers. I hope that those players in the middle refuse to listen to Mr. Canseco and eschew unnatural means of increasing their musculature, their playing statistics, or their contracts and risk their long-term health and freedom.

Older people have "assisted living." I think today we've been witnessing the era of the "assisted home run." It's never a completely clean fit to take statistics from one decade and compare them with statistics of players of another decade, but this whole business of steroids and other performance-enhancing drugs throws all of baseball's statistics out of whack. And we've now heard that baseball statistics are history. We've sullied our connection to history and our past. This is why the game has fallen off its pedestal.

When I was playing, drugs were much more "under the radar." Players were taking amphetamines or "greenies" in order to keep their energy up, not in order to transform their physiques or gain extraordinary power. They were taking stimulants not unlike an office worker drinking that extra cup of coffee to get through the afternoon. I'm not condoning drug use, not by a long shot. I never took drugs myself. I never felt I needed to. I can proudly say that I accomplished all my feats of excellence cleanly, and entered the Hall of Fame unblemished.

The owners know that it's the stars who hit the home runs who bring the fans out to the ballparks. What owner would knowingly settle for a couple of years of extra production from a star, realizing that the price was the star's future health, as well as the heated public debate of all those interested in baseball—the media backlash, the embarrassment of congressional and national scrutiny? Yes, there's no doubt in my mind that if the owners could have the last ten years back, they would be much more aggressive in policing baseball, and even their own locker rooms.

The good news today is that just about everyone in baseball recognizes the damage that drugs have caused, and everybody from the Players Association to the owners to the commissioner's office now seems to be on the same page about the importance of tackling the drug problem. A firm drug policy (one of the strongest in professional sports) is now up there with mom, the flag, and Chevrolet—it's something that everybody's for, and that's a good thing. My point is that it's not fair to blame the owners alone for a situation that everyone in baseball tolerated and used for their own success, each for their own reasons.

As long as we're talking about performance-enhancing drugs, I'll share with you very briefly what I would have done had I played in such an era: I wouldn't have taken them, pure and simple. I've been out in front on the drug issue for twenty years, ever since 1987, when I published *Turn It Around: There's No Room Here for Drugs,* my book on youth drug abuse and prevention strategies. My career was based on faith in my own abilities, to be good or bad on my own—they call that "naked." Back in my day, we weren't talking about performance-enhancing drugs. Instead, the issue was marijuana and cocaine, which could accurately be described as performance-detracting drugs. There were a few guys who "blew up" over the winter, looking buff with ten more pounds of muscle, but they weren't the top players in the game and it didn't sway people in MLB. If I didn't get involved with those drugs, I certainly would not have gotten involved with anything as risky and unproven as steroids. Instead, I would have been angry—if not outspoken—about players having a monstrous advantage by cheating—using illegal performance-enhancing drugs—affecting my ability to obtain a good contract because my drug-free performance didn't stack up to their inflated statistics.

Sometimes people ask me what I would have done had I known that a team member was "on the juice." As a player, I occasionally had the opportunity to act as confidant and discuss the issue with a teammate who had some sort of drug problem. On some of the teams for whom I played, there were guys with histories of substance abuse. My message to them was always the same: "You've got to take care of yourself. It's your life. You've got family. You can get confidential help. They are looking to bust users and high-profile players. We're trying to win over here." I can't say whether my individual interest in them or my intervention helped. It is certainly more effective to have a broad top-down policy in place to eradicate and prevent drug use.

Now that performance-enhancing drugs—at least the detectable ones—are on the decline in both the majors and minors (the testing policy was first imposed in the minor leagues), and once the George Mitchell investigation is completed, the conversation about what owners can do to improve the game of baseball can move beyond the question of illegal drugs. For instance, with their players and ballparks, there are many ways that owners can contribute to Baseball United.

The argument between the players and owners has changed. It used to be a plea on the part of the players for the owners to act with transparency, to open their books. Today, those numbers are known and shared. The size of the TV contracts, the sponsorship franchise values, and all the other critical facts and figures on the owners' balance sheets are available to the Players Association. Instead, the question has transformed into this one: "How can we find common ground? How can we work together to make baseball attractive and alluring to our fans, and more profitable for everyone?" If the owners are promoting the game one way and the players are going about it a different way, it simply doesn't work. Again, I don't want to hold up the NFL and the NBA as models of perfection. They've got their fair share of player personalities, troubles, and issues. But at the same time, they are much better at promoting their sports in a unified manner, instead of the piecemeal way that baseball does it.

Baseball teams are almost entirely owned by privately held partnerships and corporations, which means that they do not have to submit the kind of financial accounting statements that are required of publicly held corporations.

What if there hadn't been a Mark McGwire and a Sammy Sosa making joint baseball history with their buzzworthy home-run derby in 1998? What if there hadn't been a Cal Ripken Jr. breaking Lou Gehrig's record for continuous games played, demonstrating a dedication to the sport that resounded deeply with millions upon millions of hardworking Americans who show up at their jobs every day? If these individuals had not existed, would baseball have recovered from the 1994 strike year? Would the game have recovered as quickly? Hard to say, but my guess is no.

Baseball was very fortunate to have this confluence of events—

the Ripken Ironman record and the McGwire/Sosa home-run chase—to help fans move past their bitterness and disappointment over a canceled pennant race and playoffs. In the fall of 2006, baseball didn't take a chance on yet another breakdown in labor relations that could have led to another strike, but can they count on another Ripken, another McGwire/Sosa pairing to rescue the game yet again? I don't think so. That's too big a risk, and too long to wait to catch lightning in a bottle again. If there's one thing that baseball owners are capable of doing, it's measuring business risk in an intelligent fashion. I cannot think there's a single individual among them who would be willing to risk the future of the game for any one-upmanship or short-term gains. So I recommend they find a more surefire strategic method of moving forward together.

I implore the owners to act with more transparency in their financial dealings with the players and fans, and to put behind them their own internal difficulties and negativity in their dealings with the players' union. The single most important thing the owners can do to improve the standing of baseball in the minds of Americans is to reshape their relationship with the Players Association. They could even promote players and incorporate them into their marketing, contributing also to community relations in their towns. There's nothing more pressing if the game is to succeed.

Again, consider the "league think" that Pete Rozelle instilled in the minds of the owners in the NFL, or the amazing efforts that David Stern has made in his tenure as NBA commissioner to have all the owners on the same page. Not easy tasks, yet these men succeeded. Baseball needs that same sense of league think. The alternative for the industry and their fans is just too dreary to contemplate.

Another initiative in which the owners can take a lead role is making more baseball available in their communities. Owners, mark your territories! I'm sure you know that other sports have been encroaching on your most important fan base: kids. Kids today will often tell you that baseball is too slow, too boring, too hard to follow, even though more of them go to MLB games than to NFL, NBA, tennis, or soccer games. That's because it's so much easier for them to find and play games like basketball, whether it be at their local park or on TV. From October to March, it's practically impossible to turn on a TV and *not* find a basketball game being played somewhere, either live, on tape, or on a highlight show like *SportsCenter*.

Today, baseball, football, and NASCAR are ubiquitous, and soccer has proliferated as well. (And let's not forget bull riding!) If kids aren't playing those sports, they're watching them, and if they aren't involved in those sports, then they're skateboarding or playing electronic games. Baseball owners have to look beyond the rosy statistics showing how many kids are coming to the games and get a better grasp instead on the declining percentage of "mind share" that baseball possesses with young people. Baseball is not even on a lot of kids' radar. This makes no sense when you think about it, because owner after owner has spent hundreds of millions of dollars creating beautiful new ballparks, only to have MLB drop the ball when it comes to marketing initiatives, especially to the young, black, and urban communities.

Shifting all of the World Series games to nighttime greatly boosted the game's economic growth, but the decision hurt youth interest in baseball. Rare is the child who can stay up past midnight to watch the end of a World Series game, even if his parents permitted him to do so. We've taken our crown jewel, the World Series, and put it out of reach for young people. The cost of going to a game, while not quite at the stratospheric level of an NFL or NBA game, is not necessarily within the reach of every American family, especially when you consider the add-ons: parking, hot dogs, pretzels, souvenir programs. I will say it is better than the NBA or NFL, since you rarely see kids at those championship games, but you do see them at baseball games.

One of the most significant things the owners can do is to invest not just in the marketing of baseball in their regions but in the *playing* of baseball throughout their territory. The teams should devote a greater percentage of their time, money, facilities, and interest to ensure that baseball isn't just talked about or "sold" to people, but is also actually played and enjoyed by kids.

It's hard for businesspeople to put money into something where there isn't a clear return on investment. So it's difficult for me to convince all of the owners, beginning with San Diego, to spend tens or even hundreds of thousands of dollars on partnerships with local businesses, communities, and leagues to build, rebuild, and equip youth baseball facilities, to inspire quality coaching for young people (by training coaches), to make the game more accessible, and last, to be leaders in keeping baseball alive, well, and thriving in their regions. (Teams such as the Minnesota Twins and San Francisco Giants are already leaders in this area.) We're talking about a long-term payoff that is harder to quantify, or "monetize," in business-speak. Without the long-term commitment to make baseball available in every community, young people's interest in the sport will continue to wither.

If kids aren't playing baseball today, they won't be attending baseball games tomorrow. I understand that it requires long-term thinking on the part of the owners to make such an investment, but failing to do so—whether it be as part of their community relations, marketing, or team foundation efforts—will come back to haunt the game years later. There are a thousand ways to promote baseball as a game to be played and not just as a game for which tickets can be bought. There are great local programs and grassroots initiatives throughout the United States, such as Play Ball! Minnesota. Teams need to continue to share their "best practices" for attracting young people, to build upon each other's successes, and to create a huge cadre of fans, both for the present and for the future.

The most important asset of any Major League Baseball team

is not the sparkling new ballparks, because no matter how beautiful those parks may be, unless there is a winning team on the field, the fans won't come. The famous dictum from *Field of Dreams* "If you build it, he will come" is only valid for a relatively short time. The newness and excitement of a ballpark has a shockingly brief shelf life, especially when compared with the huge costs of building a park. It's not the team's home that keeps 'em coming in, it's the home team. The greatest asset of any baseball team is its players—current and retired.

It's time for owners to make greater use of these marvelous assets. Even though many of today's major leaguers play only for a short time in any given city, while they are there, these players should be outstanding ambassadors for the game. This is even more critical with former players, for whom longtime fans still feel a deep affinity. Indeed, once men reach middle age, they feel an even deeper bond to the players of their childhood than they do with current players, with whom there is often more of a cultural divide.

Players have been making far more public appearances; however, these appearances are often for an elite few, such as corporate sponsors (a trend I refer to as the "skyboxing of baseball") or the focus is on extracting the largest amount of revenue from institutions with multimillion-dollar advertising budgets by negotiating player interaction in the deals. Baseball needs to remain cognizant that the average fan will never see the inside of a luxury box or meet a player, and that while team budgets may be balanced by revenue from high-end customers like utility companies and banks, the future of the game lies with the regular Joe deciding to take his family to a baseball game on a Sunday afternoon.

Owners have to recognize the deep value of the bond between players and their fan base and of not saving all the M&M's, if you will, for the corporate fans in the luxury boxes. The fans have no idea who's in your front office, and don't care who's in your marketing department, who's in your community relations department. The only names the fans know are your players, current and former. Team owners, *make more use of these players.* Exploit these extremely valuable assets for all they are worth. Let your older fans renew their sense of connection to players of the past by bringing your retired players out for more exposure. Let younger fans have more contact with the younger players who excite them so much. This is another extremely important method by which baseball can attract and retain a fan base. *Let fans get to know and love their players.*

The team owners need to recognize that players' extraordinarily high salaries have created a wall of separation between players and fans. Players no longer live in the average community or interact with fans at the ballpark—the fans rarely see batting practices, let alone infield practices, which have virtually disappeared from the game. The only way to break that wall down is to give the fans more exposure to the players—and again, not just the superwealthy fans in the luxury boxes. Owners might respond that there's no way to force players making huge amounts of money to do public appearances. Do it this way: Let's say that a player's salary is going to be $1.5 million. Tell the player, "We'll give you $1.475 million. If you're willing to make ten personal appearances over the course of the season, we'll give you another $25,000."

The player can do the math: $2,500 an hour, just to show up and do a "grip and grin." That's a pretty good deal, and they'll take it every time. Of course, what they don't realize is that my budget for their salary was . . . $1.5 million! Other clubs use the offer at some player appearances when negotiating sponsorship deals. Maybe I'm giving away a negotiating tactic, but the point is that I'm paying them with money they would have received anyway to do something they should be doing without any extra financial incentive. Though if money is the only incentive to participate, then by all means, use it.

However you get it done, ball clubs, get it done. If you asked every owner why they went into the game of baseball, I guarantee that a good chunk of them would say it's name recognition, power, and prestige—and contact with the athletes they admire would be high on the list as well. Team ownership is a small and unique club that few can lay claim to. Take away the bank accounts, and the fans are no different than the owners. A young person who meets a player at a ballpark or in the community is never going to forget that experience, and the dollar return on both the psychological and financial investments, while difficult to quantify, is enormous.

What is the real role of owners in Baseball United? How can MLB owners play a guiding part in this comprehensive effort to reinvigorate baseball? It's pretty straightforward. The MLB owners need to recognize that it's not only about buildings or the logo or relationships with the union that controls the personalities of the game. This country is about celebrity. And it's not even about whether they're spending or not spending on this free agent or that. The most important thing that the owners can do is to recognize that while football and basketball belong to their respective leagues, baseball has always been the people's game. Fans have traditionally felt that they possessed an ownership stake both in the game of baseball as a whole and in their team. As such, fans want to feel as though they have a "seat at the table."

Yes, the fans want to come with regularity to the beautiful new ballparks sprouting up around the league, and, yes, they want to see a winning team on the field. But more than that, they—and their kids—want to feel a sense of reciprocation for all of the time, thought, effort, and dollars they lavish on the game. They want to have a sense that baseball cares about them as much as they care about baseball. They want their kids to be playing the game and loving the game. Owners can step in and make that happen with the appropriate seeding of community money. Owners can deepen the connection between players and fans by making current and former players available to meet the fans. Above all, the most important thing owners can do is reach across the bargaining table and usher in a new period of unity and goodwill between MLB, players, and fans. The game cannot thrive if owners and the union still perceive each other as bitter enemies.

Thanks to Major League Baseball, there are already some programs in place through which community groups and organizations can make requests for monies to create and augment their youth baseball initiatives. (For more information on initiatives such as the Baseball Tomorrow Fund, visit www.MLB.com.) Such funds offer grants for the purpose of helping children enjoy baseball in areas where the game might not otherwise be available. The Baseball Tomorrow Fund grants, for example, build capacity, improve or expand existing programs, and promote and enhance the growth of baseball in the United States and throughout the world.

I reached out not too long ago to Yankees owner George Steinbrenner. Any baseball fan whose recollections go back to the 1980s certainly remembers the difficult relationship that he and I had after I came to the Yankees. I won't rehash that history now, but it was a painful time for me in many ways. George and I had not spoken in quite some time, although he'd privately given me his personal apologies, and then even held a Dave Winfield Day at Yankee Stadium in 2001. We've been able to interact, throw out first pitches, attend Old Timer's Game, and we've even shared plans for the new Yankee Stadium and its fan-friendly components. In essence, we have put the past behind us, collaborating in order to improve baseball. If Dave Winfield and George Steinbrenner can get along, anything in this game is possible.

CHAPTER 3

The New Color Line

In 1947, Jackie Robinson became the first African American to compete at the major league level in more than half a century when he crossed the color line and began his career with the Brooklyn Dodgers. Until that moment, with the exception of a handful of Native American and light-complexioned Latin players, there had not been a single ballplayer of color in the major leagues since baseball's early days, in the late 1880s.

Sixty years later, in 2006, in the finals of the inaugural World Baseball Classic, teams from Korea, Japan, Cuba, and the Dominican Republic competed at San Diego's Petco Park. What struck me as I watched the games was that there was not a single Caucasian baseball player on any team. The fans didn't seem to mind, and they loved the competition on TV and in person. The men played some good, fervent team baseball, with Japan emerging as the champion.

Obviously, society and the game of baseball have both changed. From 1947, when Jackie Robinson joined the Dodgers, until 2006, when an all-Asian team competed with an all-Hispanic team for a world championship, a major shift had taken place. The rest of the world had caught up with us. America was eliminated even before the finals. Yet there is another change happening within the game of baseball with regard to ethnicity and race, and we all need to be aware of it.

The shift that's occurring has to do with the fact that fewer African Americans are making it to the major league level, while an increasing number of Latin American ballplayers have come to dominate the game. White American participation remains pretty constant, international players from Korea to Australia are coming up as well. There's nothing wrong with this; I'm all for every athlete having an equal opportunity to develop talents and compete for a spot at the major league level. But my sense is that few people in or out of baseball are aware of the reasons behind this shift in demographics. People often ask me why this ethnic and racial transformation in American baseball has occurred. The transformation is not unlike other major American businesses where outsourcing becomes a more viable and cost-effective business approach. Because it is important that baseball consider its stance on this change, in addition to its responsibilities in the always delicate and complicated world of race and culture, I will attempt to address this issue.

First, let's consider the situation facing African American players and baseball. From 1946 to the 1970s, the number of African Americans in the game was consistently on the rise. One by one, teams desegregated (Boston was last, in 1957 with Pumpsie Green), and baseball as a whole grew in terms of quality of play and excitement for the fans. Hank Aaron, Willie Mays, Willie McCovey, Don Newcombe, Willie Stargell, and myriad other African American players left an indelible mark on the game, setting new standards, breaking records, and welcoming a new generation of African Americans into major league ballparks.

A combination of factors, however, has reduced the number of African American players in baseball, from a peak of 28 percent of all players on major league rosters in 1975 down to just 8 percent in 2006. The average per team was three, and fewer of them are stars than ever before. Indeed, on the 2005 Houston Astros, there were times when the team had only one African American player. Charles Gipson and Charlton Jimerson both played briefly for the Astros during the regular season that year, but neither played during the postseason. The 2005 Astros were the first team since the 1953 Yankees to play in the World Series without a single African American.

So where have all the African American players—and fans—gone?

First, other college and major league sports, most notably football and basketball, have siphoned away the interest of young African American athletes, who, like their peers, see baseball's competitors as more lucratively viable, whether playing in college or the pros. Most kids, parents, and their communities have subscribed to the mind-set that money, fame, opportunity, and acceptance are more accessible in football and basketball than in baseball.

In the African American community, basketball is the game to play and football is the game to watch, in part because of the riches and glory that await the chosen few who develop into NBA and NFL players. Hip, tough NBA players have become the heroes and icons for younger generations, a fact that sports marketing has capitalized on. (Take LeBron James's shoe contract money, for example.) NFL players and the NFL's product marketing also have successfully introduced the glorified football hero image into the African American community.

(The irony is that many of today's basketball heroes have yet to win a championship, and unless they get some better players around them, they might go through their entire careers without a ring. This won't hurt them any when it comes to fame or endorsements, which used to be restricted primarily to players who actually *won* something. It reminds me of what Magic Johnson said about a young Shaquille O'Neal, who was making movies and recording rap albums before he had come close to winning his first NBA championship: "Before you can be the *man,* you've got to be *the man.* "Meaning, before you go around collecting glory, go earn some!)

Also, a basketball court is relatively inexpensive to maintain and requires little space, an important consideration in urban neighborhoods. Today, when real estate development has claimed so much of the green spaces in our cities and suburbs, it is increasingly difficult and expensive to maintain baseball diamonds, especially when you compare them with the minimal maintenance necessary to maintain a basketball court. With a basketball court, there's no outfield to mow weekly, no base paths to protect, no pitcher's mound to groom, no need for bases, foul lines drawn for every game, backstops, or any of the expensive gear— gloves, balls, bats, catchers' masks, chest protectors, shin guards, and so on. Basketball games practically take care of themselves, plus you need only a few people—two will do—to play. You can even work up a sweat shooting by yourself. In comparison, even pickup baseball games that can be played with as few as two players are becoming lost activities, and rounding up the ideal number of eighteen friends to play a game of softball or baseball is a major undertaking.

Kids can't wear baseball spikes to school but basketball sneakers are permitted—so promotions for basketball win out by default. But many basketball fans are familiar with basketball shoe brands, travel leagues like the AAU, the unofficial "agents," and the rest of the hangers-on who are aware of practically every young prospect in the country, no matter how young, no matter how poor. Football maintains its own elaborate scouting systems, both official and unofficial, whereby fledgling talent is tracked from an early age.

Unbeknownst to most urban-dwelling parents, the equivalent to these systems has evolved in the past ten years for baseball players. Yes, amateur websites (such as www.baseballamerica.com) track prospects at the junior high and high school levels, but they're nowhere near as comprehensive or popular as those for other sports. If you play basketball and you're good, your neighborhood knows about you, the surrounding community knows about you, and thanks to the Internet, everyone with the slightest interest in basketball knows all about you. Less so for baseball.

One such young basketball prospect, Sebastian Telfair, who, as I write, plays for the Boston Celtics, was the subject of a nonfiction book and a documentary film, both of which tracked his basketball career even before his teenage years. Where are the baseball-playing Sebastian Telfairs? Where are the books and movies about upcoming young baseball stars? There aren't any.

And then there's the question of college. Typically, basketball and football programs offer large numbers of full scholarships to players who can quickly achieve national prominence in the NCAA men's basketball tournament in March when they play for an entire month with high national TV ratings, or on nationally televised football games culminating in the BCS Bowls. Baseball's College World Series wasn't even televised when I played in 1973. Although today the College World Series is a staple of ESPN, only a small fraction of the people who tune in to the bowls and March Madness even know that the College World Series exists, let alone could tell you when or where it takes place. (For the record, it's played in Omaha, Nebraska, in June.) And even as one who participated in it, I'm almost hurt by the marketing term "the road to Omaha"—the average sports fan is highly unlikely to be aware that anything of importance takes place in Nebraska (no disrespect intended to my Cornhusker readers), but a quarter of a million people trek to the Nebraskan city for the series each year.

Even if he somehow overcomes the fact that there are relatively few baseball diamonds in the inner city, and even if he opts for baseball over other sports, the potential college baseball player still has to figure out how to pay for college. That's because very few schools offer more than half scholarships to their baseball-playing athletes, simply because there's not enough money to be made from college baseball, compared with the immensely more lucrative college sports of basketball and football. If you are a young African American and you're athletic, chances are that baseball isn't going to be your first-choice sport.

The NCAA dictates how many scholarships its colleges and universities are permitted per sport. These total scholarship numbers can be divided among different athletes; for example, two athletes might get half scholarships and that would be counted as one. Division 1A football teams are allowed to offer eighty-five scholarships. Division 1AA football teams can offer sixty-three scholarships, which can be divided up among a maximum of eighty-five athletes.

Other college sports don't fare nearly as well. Women's basketball teams can offer fifteen scholarships or equivalencies thereof; men's basketball, thirteen; women's volleyball and women's gymnastics, twelve; and men's baseball, only 11.7. The fewer the scholarships, the fewer the places for lower-income athletes, and inner-city African Americans more often than not fall into that category. Of the major sports, only women's tennis receives fewer scholarships (eight) than men's baseball.

But let's say baseball is your game. Let's say that you grew up idolizing a Derek Jeter or a Gary Sheffield, or, if you're "old school" enough or know your recent history, maybe even a Winfield or a Reggie Jackson. If this description fits you, and it fits a decreasing number of African American athletes every year, the next step is to have Major League Baseball pay attention to you. They'll know who you are with the help of technology, Major League Baseball scouts, camps, showcases, and other outlets, but can they afford to draft you? Only a limited number may be drafted, and I'll tell you why:

1. Few teams are scouting the urban markets because many baseball diamonds in urban areas are broken, unsafe, or far behind the standards of more sophisticated leagues and games.

2. MLB teams are drafting skilled players who are further along in their development, and not as many raw players who are still several years away from the MLB.

3. There are more kids going to college than ever before, and for decades, few African Americans have played baseball on scholarship or as walk-ons.

This is the way the baseball draft operates: A first-round draft choice is subject to rules and expectations about signing bonuses and salaries. A top-quality baseball prospect from the United States is going to cost a team three or four million dollars to draft and sign. Matt Young, for example, several years ago received a multimillion-dollar signing bonus. Even a quality player not picked in the first round with a decent chance of making it to the majors is still a million-dollar gamble. This is where the issues of money collide.

If you were the owner of a major league team, you would have learned over the past twenty-plus years to hedge your bets on foreign-born Latin players by building academies in these countries to scout, sign, and teach young talent. The rules there are different for signing—the age is younger—and it's less expensive. It's a safe bet to sign twenty Latin American ballplayers who have done nothing but eat, sleep, dream, and play baseball all their lives.

The rapid decline—indeed, the plummeting numbers—of African American players does not in any way reflect a resurgence of racism on the part of Major League Baseball. Far from it. If you're a four- or five-tool player, or even if you're really good at one particular aspect of the game—defense, hitting, pitching, and so on—and you've gone through this system I'm telling you about, you will be seen, scouted, rated, put in the MLB scouting system, or be offered a college scholarship. It doesn't matter if you're black, white, or purple with pink polka dots. There's a place on a major league roster for you. But it takes more money today to go through the process. It simply comes down to economics. You've got far fewer African American kids playing baseball, and it simply makes little economic sense to throw a ton of money at one single player—especially since only a few even make it through the system to the major leagues—when you can spend the same amount on twenty players from overseas.

The following story will explain why you've seen the proliferation of Latin players in far greater numbers in Major League Baseball than you see in society, college, TV, or anywhere else.

Let's look at the numbers. In 1946, Jackie Robinson received $3,500 from the Brooklyn Dodgers to play Major League Baseball. In 1986, Sammy Sosa signed his first major league contract—and he received the exact same amount of money. Major League Baseball has developed what has been called a "boatload mentality" toward Latin American players: The teams can buy a boatload of players for the same amount of money it costs to sign one player born in the United States. That's because the rules regarding signing bonuses for players born in the United States simply do not apply to those born outside our borders. Let's take a look at some examples of this phenomenon.

In 1996, Miguel Tejada came from the Dominican Republic to play baseball and received a signing bonus of $2,000. That same year, Matt White signed for a $10.2 million bonus as an amateur free agent with the Tampa Bay Devil Rays. You've probably never heard of Matt White, but Tejada turned out to be a good gamble. The As got a lot of good years out of him before he broke the bank with free agency to the Baltimore Orioles. It's not racism; it's just smart business sense.

The problem is that ballplayers from the inner city, who can't afford college on half scholarship, are far less likely to have a shot at that big bonus money than their counterparts from middle- and upper-class homes. And if they can't compete in college, they are less likely to develop the tools and skills necessary to be drafted. Even if they qualified for the draft, simple economics dictates that you look not to America's inner cities for your future stars but to the Dominican Republic, Panama, Venezuela, and other points south.

At age eleven, Tejada quit school to work full time in the sugar-cane fields of his native Dominican Republic, and he was homeless for many years during his quest to make it to the majors, so he was always highly motivated to succeed. Tejada is not alone—it is the dream of practically every young man in many Latin American nations to make it as a ballplayer. Indeed, there are few other career options, aside from working in agriculture. The question that arises, and one that Major League Baseball has been facing directly in recent years, is the means by which we are locating, training, schooling, and bringing these players to the United States for their shot at a career.

It's a complex situation, to say the least. According to the Northwestern University *Journal of International Human Rights,* "In 2000, the Cleveland Indians signed forty Latin American ballplayers for approximately $700,000. Their first draft pick, an 18-year-old pitcher from the United States, was paid more than one million dollars above that price."* There's nothing wrong with a business seeking to find, develop, and import talent. This occurs in countless professional fields, from nursing to software engineers. There's also nothing wrong with seeking to find the best talent at the best price. And yet, Major League Baseball's desire to find prospects in other nations is overshadowed by the complicated economic, political, and military history that the United States shares with these nations.

In other words, the development of baseball players in Latin America doesn't occur in a historical vacuum. Even though you've seen and rooted for the success stories of players like Sammy Sosa, David Ortiz, and the hundreds before them like Juan Marichal, Orlando Cepeda, and Roberto Clemente, the

---

* www.law.northwestern.edu/journals/jihr/v4/n2/6.

process behind obtaining these players has not always been something to be proud of.

The process for locating prospects south of the border used to be fairly simple: American scouts would travel the back roads of Latin and South American nations, visiting towns and villages, watching boys play ball and talking to their network of local contacts for information about who could hit well and who could pitch. Teams would then sign individual players, often for a pittance. As the salary structure in baseball changed, the value of young Latin prospects also grew. A cadre of semiofficial scouts, known as *buscones,* came into existence in the Dominican Republic. They took it upon themselves to develop their own scouting networks and to locate boys still in the midst of their adolescence. In exchange for a trifling sum of money, which still dwarfed the income of the boy's father, the buscones would become responsible for connecting the young player with one of the many teams that crisscrossed the Dominican Republic looking for talent.

In recent years, buscones have come under enormous criticism because many of them have taken huge percentages of signing bonuses and salaries as part of their agreements with the players, and the system is rife with abuse. If the buscones are the providers of talent, on the receiving end are the American baseball teams, which have developed "baseball academies" in the Dominican Republic, where these boys are sent.

The term *buscon* derives from a Spanish word meaning "searcher" or "finder." Buscones take as much as 40 percent of the signing bonuses for funding the young players they represent. Since Major League Baseball has no jurisdiction to regulate the buscones, these "finders" will sign kids (under their own brand of personal services agreement) as young as twelve and thirteen years of age, providing them with shoes, a glove, and spikes, gear their families couldn't possibly afford. Some buscones will actually hide their players in distant parts of the Dominican Republic, to keep them from the eyes of certain American scouts or teams.

The classic story of buscon abuse is that of Enrique Soto, often referred to as the "king of the buscones" in the Dominican Republic, and Willy Aybar, a player who grew up in dire poverty, living "six to a room, in a concrete-and-tin house on the Bani River—a watery dump filled with garbage and raw sewage. He taught himself to hit using whittled branches that he kept in a special corner of his room."* When the Los Angeles Dodgers signed him with a $1.4 million signing bonus—the most ever paid to a Dominican player—Aybar knew so little of finances that he was unaware that he had to sign the back of the check in order to cash it. Aybar's mother says that out of the almost $500,000 of the initial payment, the family only saw a lump-sum payment of $6,250 and a monthly stipend of less than $2,000. Soto paid the agent who negotiated Aybar's contract $35,000, and allegedly kept the rest of the money—about $430,000—for himself.

Some buscones have their own first-class training facilities and coaching staffs, while others scramble to provide equipment, facilities, and training for their players. It has also been alleged that buscones have given their young charges steroids, often just days before tryouts with big league teams, and provided them with false birth certificates, either to show that a player is old enough to be signed by Major League Baseball or legal but young enough to get a large paycheck. The buscones understand that a younger ballplayer is worth more in the marketplace than an older one, and they allegedly encourage the players to use birth certificates and identities of relatives or other community members who have died.

It's not fair to say that baseball is turning a blind eye to these practices. Baseball is aware of what goes on in the Dominican Republic, but it would be a gross exaggeration to say that Major League Baseball has solved these problems. The system may not

* Steve Fainaru, "The Business of Building Ballplayers," *The Washington Post,* June 17, 2001.

be respectable, but it does provide a steady stream of less expensive talent.

If a Dominican youngster has the slightest amount of baseball talent, he will dream of making it to one of the baseball academies run in his country by some of the major league teams, such as the Yankees, As, or the Dodgers. A boy who is tapped for a baseball academy will quit school at a young age, often as early as twelve, all but destroying his ability to earn a living at anything other than cutting sugarcane, should his dream of a professional baseball career not pan out. For these young men, it is truly all or nothing. Only a small percentage of the boys who make it to the baseball academies are legitimate prospects; the rest are decent players—fillers or backups—with no shot at a major league career (but no one tells them that). They are present only to fill out rosters, so that the true prospects can have teams of adequate size in order to develop their skills.

The baseball academies ostensibly provide educational opportunities for the boys, but the reality has been that the curriculum is baseball around the clock. The boys are constantly playing, practicing, or learning about the game. Of the prospects who make it to the baseball academies, only a small number will be offered contracts and a shot in the minor leagues. Their road will not be an easy one, as they will arrive in the United States with limited English, no experience with American culture, and often intense homesickness as they are dispersed to minor league teams around the country.

These young men in their late teens have more than likely been sent to a community that lacks a substantial Spanish-speaking population. Today, some teams are providing English lessons to prospects, but they remain isolated, lonely, ill at ease, and unable to communicate. Under these circumstances, they must prove themselves to an impatient baseball establishment that will discard them if they do not appear to be developing quickly enough. From their ranks will emerge the individuals good enough to make it to the majors, and of those ballplayers, a few will become legitimate major league stars. Those who succeed at the highest levels will do extremely well. The top one hundred Latin American ballplayers earned *$525 million* in salary in the year 2005; the other nearly 140 players earned a minimum of about $325,000 each.

Half a billion dollars divided up among just a hundred ballplayers indicates the level of astonishing financial success that awaits the best of the best. But not everyone can make it to the majors (though in the minors, a young man can make a living as well). There's a funnel, and only a very small percentage of those who make it even as far as the baseball academies will ever see the inside of a major league ballpark. Those who fail in the minors return home disheartened, broken, injured, perhaps in disgrace, with no other career options. Many remain in the United States as undocumented aliens, still lacking language skills, hoping to find a way to make it now that baseball is no longer an option.

The way the process works means that for every legitimate major league player who is a product of the baseball academies, there are hundreds more who quit school in order to have a shot, no matter how remote, at the big time and big money. An obvious question is whether we are truly doing right by these individuals and their communities, especially those boys who are brought to the baseball academies just to fill out the rosters. The process has been be compared to strip mining: We are shearing away these nations' most valuable resources, the futures of their young men, in exchange for an elusive and all too often illusory shot at Major League Baseball glory. Is it fair? Is it right? Is there a better way?

If you're an adolescent or a teenager playing baseball anywhere in the United States and you're good, you'll be seen and people will hear about you. This goes for players in high school as well as any organized league such as Babe Ruth or American Legion ball. American players cannot be signed until they finish high school or turn seventeen; if they enter college, they can only be signed after their junior year. Long before that point, though, you'll come to the attention of a bird dog, a regional checker, a scouting bureau—someone will have seen you.

The teams put their draft "wish lists" together in meetings with their general managers and scouts. There are thirty teams and fifty rounds in the annual baseball draft. Those athletes chosen in the first round will receive bonuses from a million dollars up to four million dollars. It's a risky proposition to give that kind of money to an unproven high school student, but for a college athlete who has developed some maturity through education, travel, and competition, it's often not a bad bet. They are, in theory, closer to being ready to play in MLB.

Players who go in the second round receive signing bonuses of half a million to a million dollars. A third-round signing bonus is smaller, and later rounds are lower still. Many athletes will sign out of high school because college is not for them, or they think they won't be drafted in an early round later on, if at all. Kids who are good want to get drafted because they expect they will get more money, will be given a longer look if they have been drafted, and thus will have more opportunity to succeed.

Outside the United States, the rules are different, thus allowing for the buscones to do what they do. The rules say that Major League Baseball cannot sign a prospect born outside the United States until he turns sixteen, but there are always exceptions. Nailing down the precise age of a young player is not always an easy task.

The teams have begun to consider their responsibilities to the various Latin American communities where they search for players. While baseball has not addressed in any meaningful way its relationship with the buscones, it has begun to do a better job in terms of the facilities and the education and life skills that are taught at the baseball academies. The Yankees and Dodgers have been in the lead. The other teams are not far behind and, I'm pleased to report, among them are the San Diego Padres, who are now investing millions of dollars in their academy in the Dominican Republic, purchasing their own property, seeking quality, trustworthy coaching and management, and providing living conditions for the young players that will be quite good.

The owner, John Moores, visited Dominican facilities and saw conditions he deemed deplorable, and is determined to revamp the entire academy. He and the front office in San Diego want the team to forge a great reputation in the Dominican Republic and to be perceived as a desirable organization for which to play. So it makes sense to the Padres to make that kind of investment, and other teams are either considering it or already doing the same.

Even with the advent of baseball academies and the growing concern for the role—and often the greed—of the buscones, can Major League Baseball truly be said to be meeting its responsibilities to the Latin American communities from which it extracts its prospects? Or is the strip mining analogy still appropriate? Now that this practice, along with other issues, has come to light, baseball needs to operate with a high level of sensitivity for the fact that most of those young people are statistically unlikely to achieve the wealth and success of the chosen few who make it to the majors. By sifting through dozens, hundreds, even thousands of prospects to find that one major league–level player, we are inducing thousands of young men each year to halt their studies in pursuit of the baseball dream.

Is it good business for Major League Baseball to look for talent in other countries, to pursue relationships with Australia, Japan, China, and Korea and not just Latin America? Of course. I hope we'll just be as cognizant of the potential problems and do it the right way.

Put it all together and you end up with a situation where, as our culture and society has evolved, it is economically unfeasible for baseball to attract and promote increasing numbers of young African American players. The kids don't have access to baseball diamonds, strong leagues, or quality coaching. The scholarship money may not be there if they're interested in pursuing baseball on the college level. There are fewer and fewer African American role models in the majors to point the way. The best athletes in the community are being influenced by other activities and stolen from baseball, unlike fifty or even thirty years ago, when the best athletes played baseball. At the same time, a rising number of Latin American ballplayers are competing for that severely limited number of openings on major league teams. Thus the shift in the racial and ethnic makeup of the game today, and why almost 30 percent of Major League Baseball players, and more than 40 percent in the minor leagues, are Latin American, while less than one in ten is African American.

If I thought baseball was racist in its policies of finding and promoting players, I'd say so here. I just don't think that's the case. Baseball is a business, as we are endlessly reminded, and countless businesses today are going offshore to find their workforces. Baseball is no different.

Jimmie Lee Solomon, senior vice president of baseball operations for Major League Baseball, was ranked ninth by *Sports Illustrated* among the 101 most influential members of minority groups and sports and he is committed to raising baseball's profile. He handles special projects like the All-Star Futures Game showcasing minor league prospects, the Reviving Baseball in the Inner City (RBI) Program, the MLB Urban Youth Academy, and the Minority Umpire Scholarship program. So don't let anybody tell you baseball isn't already taking steps toward increasing the number of African Americans in the game, at every level. I'm just saying I believe we can do more, and we can do it more quickly.

The Latin American player may find a lot of peers once he reaches the higher minor leagues and the major league level, but baseball is still lagging in terms of respect for the contribution of the Latin American ballplayer. When baseball created its All-

Century team to honor the best of the best of the twentieth-century ballplayers, not one Latin American player made the team. The closest was Roberto Clemente, who came in tenth, behind Pete Rose, in a ranking of the best outfielders. Baseball belatedly remedied that embarrassment by creating an all-Latin All-Star team, and then in 2006, Clemente was honored with the highest baseball award at the All-Star Game in Pittsburgh, accepted by his wife, Vera Clemente, on his behalf.

Over the last decade, some young ballplayers have been so desperate for an edge that will catapult them out of poverty and into the major league level that they will inject or ingest practically anything they think might help. There have even been stories of the use of animal steroids. In similar circumstances, major league players who have proven track records of success at the highest level often receive second, third, fourth, and fifth chances. By comparison, young Latin players have no reputation and no one to fight for them when they are faced with lengthy or career-ending suspensions for their steroid use.

I would strongly advocate that Major League Baseball present a more complete picture to young Latin players that lays out exactly what their chances are, exactly what they may expect if they are fortunate enough to come to the United States to play, and what the pitfalls are, as well as how to avoid them. Baseball also must find ways to get its antisteroid message into these communities and find a way to counter the idea that you can ease your path to the majors by taking drugs. One possibility is for baseball to make greater use of its Latin American stars by employing them as mentors to young players, both here in the United States and in their home countries.

My intention is not to question the morality of seeking out talent wherever it can be found, and I am all for every Latin American ballplayer receiving his chances to make it to the majors, just as every African American player in this country ought to receive his due. At the same time, baseball has to better address the question of the disappearing African American ballplayer. The opening in spring 2006 of the first baseball academy in inner-city Compton, California, is a great positive step. But it's up to Major League Baseball and American communities to ensure its success and to create other baseball academies across the nation.

As I mentioned earlier, after many years of planning and preparation, MLB's first Urban Youth Baseball Academy was unveiled in 2006. The ten-million-dollar facility, made possible through combined contributions from Major League Baseball clubs, spans ten acres on the campus of Compton Community College in South Los Angeles. It provides fields for practice and instruction for boys and girls. The facility also offers an educational after-school component—seminars and clinics by former players and health classes.

The baseball academy is designed for children from eight to eighteen. It recently added youth fields for T-ball leagues and sandlot-type games like whiffle ball, T-ball, stickball, and strike-out for children ages five to seven years old. That's the prime age when kids first start learning to love the game. It would be great if major league teams could find some space around their ballparks where kids could play these same games. That would be a terrific building block for learning and loving the game.

I've developed a close relationship with Jimmie Lee Solomon, the MLB executive who launched the academy, and with Darrell Miller, the director of the baseball academy in Compton. The facility will be providing the faculty, mentors, and teaching tools needed to expose young kids to the requisite baseball education to compete and perhaps succeed in the highly competitive workplace called Major League Baseball. This can help ensure the future of baseball in the inner city . . . and the future of many African American players in the game of baseball.

There's not a single living African American ballplayer of Jackie Robinson's generation who could possibly have imagined that within his lifetime, the sacrifices that Robinson and others made would appear almost futile and that the fervor for the game and the flame that burned for decades is now only flickering. If there are few African American players, then there will be fewer African American fans, and interest among African Americans in the game will continue to drop. The game of baseball is approaching that tipping point. I don't think that's a future that anyone in baseball would like to see.

I therefore would like to propose that Major League Baseball create Jackie Robinson grants (supported in part by corporate grants, fund-raising efforts, or even an annual benefit affair), which would create funds available to African Americans who receive baseball scholarships to NCAA institutions. I'm not looking to create any kind of quota system or to "reverse an imbalance." Rather, I think it's important for baseball to recognize just how hard—even how unlikely—it has become for an inner-city African American to connect with the game of baseball, choose it over other sports, and reach a level of proficiency sufficient that he would be selected for a scholarship by an NCAA institution. This in and of itself is a remarkable accomplishment and something that we ought to applaud . . . and encourage.

In any given year, the number of inner-city student-athletes earning baseball scholarships is going to be very small. So the actual financial investment required by Major League Baseball to make this a reality would be equally small. But talk about bang for the buck: If an African American teen from an inner-city neighborhood or economically disadvantaged background knows that MLB will provide funds to accompany his scholarship money—in essence, a matching grant—that young man is much more likely to accept the baseball scholarship, even a partial one, to play baseball in college, and to pursue a major league career.

Along with the Jackie Robinson grants, I propose a mentorship program, to match not just African American ballplayers, but any interested college student, with major league players or MLB alumni who can serve as instructors or big brothers. One of the themes that runs through this book is that baseball is the hardest game to learn to play, and the process of learning the mental aspect of the game takes many years longer than any other professional sport. It would be tremendous if young athletes had an opportunity to meet major leaguers, not in an autograph session or a grip-and-grin public relations event, but instead in a mentoring relationship where they would meet or communicate on a regular, ongoing basis to learn the facts, techniques, and lore of the game.

It's one thing—and it's a great thing—to write a check to support a compelling cause. It's even better when there is person-to-person contact. Even at the college level, most ballplayers still don't understand exactly what it takes to make it to the majors. Who better to tell them than a major leaguer himself? The Jackie Robinson grants would go a long way toward creating a pool of talented African American baseball prospects who might not otherwise have a chance to develop to the major league level. Combine that with a mentoring program made up of current and former major leaguers, and you can develop an enormous amount of passion and excitement for the game.

Finally, I propose that MLB initiates an annual series of town hall meetings that reach inner-city high schools, colleges, park and recreation departments, and parents and kids in an effort to provide better understanding of the aspects of the sport we are discussing here. This will go a long way toward providing information and the motivation to stay involved and reach for the ring.

CHAPTER 4

The Last Black Major Leaguer

In 1975, 28 percent of the baseball players in the major leagues were African American. Today, that percentage has dwindled down to *8 percent.* In other words, in thirty years, the number of African American major league baseball players has plummeted.

Based on this downward trajectory, the percentage of African Americans in baseball could drop to below 1 percent in just ten short years. It's reasonable to think that the percentage has bottomed out and therefore won't continue to decline so steeply, but let's assume for a moment that the trend will continue apace.

What exactly would that mean? Two things. First, it means that from when Jackie Robinson broke the color line in Major League Baseball in 1947 to the appearance of the last African American major league player is a period of approximately seventy-five years. Not one African American player of Robinson's generation or mine could have imagined such a turn of events.

It also means that the last African American Major League Baseball player, the very last one to reach The Show, is twelve years old as you read these words.

He's out there somewhere. We don't know exactly where, and we don't know exactly which twelve-year-old African American it will be, but it might be interesting to take a look at baseball history and American sociology, economics, and history to determine where that young man might be found. We don't know exactly what region of the country is home to this young man, but chances are, he lives somewhere in the South or the Southwest. When a lake dries up, there are still places where water covers the earth, where the soil is still fertile underneath—and so it is with baseball. Even as the game has dried up in many parts of the country, there are still places where it endures. These locales are primarily in the Sunbelt and Southern states, where kids can play outside for most of the year.

It's not likely that our young man hails from the inner city, because as we have seen, spaces for playing the game in urban areas no longer exist. It's simply not safe to allow children to play unsupervised in many of those communities, and government money isn't there to provide adequate facilities. Chances are our young man comes from a prosperous part of the nation, a community affluent enough to provide great baseball facilities, club teams, and leagues for its kids: well-maintained diamonds, fields that are mown, if not manicured, and the equipment for playing the game.

Another reason why our young man is not likely to come from an inner-city background is that, sad to say, inner-city kids may not have that much contact with their father. There is a higher percentage of single-parent homes in the inner city. Without a father or grandfather with whom to play catch and to have the knowledge of the game passed on to him, a young man in the inner city is far more likely to turn to basketball or football. The facilities are there, his friends are playing the game, and, if his father is around, odds are that his father favors basketball or football as well. (This current generation of dads didn't play much baseball, either.)

Our young man may well be the son of a Major League Baseball player. It takes a lot of money to live in a nice suburb, and Dad may well have earned the money to pay for their lifestyle as a professional player himself. Ideally, a baseball player is so exciting to watch, so athletic, so fluid in his movements that any young athlete should be excited by the game.

When I see young athletes moving in slow motion on a baseball diamond, I ask myself, Where's the style? Where's the "wow factor" that inspires awe in the fans? I wish young African Americans could see that baseball offers as much opportunity for exquisite play-making as do other sports, but that lesson is becoming increasingly harder to convey.

Our young man has most likely developed his interest in baseball without much assistance from the African American media. In days gone by, baseball and boxing were pretty much the only sports that African American newspapers covered. Back in the day, there was a symbiotic relationship between the Negro Leagues and black-owned newspapers across the country. The coverage of baseball in African American newspapers helped increase the popularity of the sport among African Americans nationwide and created a hunger to see African Americans in the major leagues that was only satisfied in 1947, when Jackie Robinson broke the color line.

Our young man may never have seen an African American newspaper in his life. If he did, and he turned to the sports pages, he would see coverage of basketball and football, but not all that much about baseball. If you ask editors of African American newspapers why they stopped writing about baseball, they'd tell you that besides a weekly publishing schedule, having staffs too small to send someone to major league ballparks, where there aren't enough black players for ball games to be worthwhile covering, it's also because people stopped caring about the game. This is a chicken-and-egg question: Did the people stop caring, and therefore the newspaper writers stopped writing? Or did the newspapers stop writing about baseball, and therefore people stopped caring?

However you look at it, our young man won't have gleaned much about baseball from African American media. If his parents happen to subscribe to *Ebony* magazine, he would no longer see the photographs, team by team, of all the African Americans in the major leagues. A decade or two ago, *Ebony* halted the practice of showing all the African Americans on each team in both leagues. I remember seeing those photographs and feeling a sense of pride. It made me think that there might be a place for me in Major League Baseball.

Before 1947, when there were no players of color in Major League Baseball, the game wasn't at its best. The quality of play improved when African Americans entered the major leagues— I don't think there's a single baseball historian who would dispute that point. And without African Americans, it will revert to a state where the game is no longer at its best. The game won't be as good as it can be if African Americans are not represented on the playing field.

By the time our young man becomes a teenager, there will be so few African Americans in the major leagues that he won't have that same affinity toward the game that I had. His love for the game more than likely comes from his father because his friends, African American and otherwise, are more likely to play basketball, football, or soccer. They probably think baseball is too slow, boring, or out of step with their cool, urban, hip-hop, tough-talking mentality.

Does our young friend even know who Jackie Robinson was? He probably has no inkling that his name and Robinson's will be forever linked, Robinson as the first African American major leaguer seventy-five years before him, and our young friend, the last one. If he's heard of Robinson at all, it may not be because he's interested in sports, but simply because Robinson is a part of American history. The only problem is that most kids don't really fancy themselves as history buffs. It's not likely that he's going to spend much time reading up on the history of the Negro Leagues.

He may never have heard of the Negro Leagues at all, for that matter. He may never have heard of Satchel Paige, Josh Gibson, or, as I mentioned earlier, even John "Buck" O'Neil, Willie Mays, Monte Irvin, and Hank Aaron, individuals who played in the Negro Leagues and/or excelled in the majors. Has he ever heard of Rickey Henderson or Dave Winfield? I'd like to think he has. Maybe his mom or dad knew the names.

There's a very high likelihood that the young man will play on traveling teams and in showcase games. By the time he's in his early teens, his skills will have become so well developed that colleges and even professional scouts will be aware of him. He will develop the instincts and knowledge of the game so necessary for a young player to compete in college and pro ball. As he moves up through the ranks past Little League, he will see fewer and fewer faces of color. The higher he rises, the fewer fellow African Americans he will encounter. Although America is growing and experiencing a demographic shift, it is likely that when he goes on the road with the traveling teams, with his college and minor league teams, he will be visiting towns and cities with few black faces. This may not be as difficult an adjustment for our young man as one might expect, because he has been living in an affluent, suburban community for his entire life, and the number of African Americans in his circle will almost certainly be limited. It will still be a difficult adjustment for him to be away from home, away from his family's culture, and in clubhouses where he will invariably be the only African American.

His experience will not be like Jackie Robinson's, in that Jackie came along at a time of avowed racism in our society, when bigots were not afraid to step up and tell you how they felt about you. Instead, our young man will sense that he is the object of curiosity ranging from idle to intense, not just on the part of his fellow ballplayers and coaches, but also with those who attend the games. Will they recognize how hard he has worked to attain the level of talent, skill, and grace he displays? Or will those around him chalk up his talent to "natural ability," assuming that because he is African American, he is simply good at sports? They'll never say, and he'll never know.

Major league clubhouses sometimes segregate themselves even today along racial and ethnic lines. Will he feel lonely as the only African American in the clubhouse? What will he have to do to fit in? Will he feel entitled to display his full range of emotions, as the other players do, or will he fear that he will be stereotyped as an angry black player? Will he have to throttle aspects of his personality in order to fit in? Will more or less be expected of him because of his race? Will coaches and managers afford him the same opportunities to succeed as the other players? Or will they feel justified in making negative decisions regarding his career? If he starts to falter or go into a slump, will he be benched more quickly than other players might be, or will he be given a full opportunity to play himself back into the winning column?

As the last African American baseball player, he'll make good money during his time whether he is a starter, a star, or a bench-warmer. He'll go down in history, no matter what he does. Obviously, I'm hoping that it never comes to this. But if it does, I wish that young man a productive career, and a very long run. The day he disappears from baseball, after two decades of productivity, after a few years of mediocrity, after a career-ending injury, or even after the proverbial "cup of coffee," something within each of the African American players who have preceded him will vanish, too—that sense of hope that was instilled in us by the Negro Leaguers and the first black major leaguers for countless generations of African American players to come. Not just three generations. Not just three and out. That's not why they did what they did. That's not why my generation did what we did.

When our young player looks out into the stands at any level of competition, from the parents at his Little League games to the crowded stands of a major league park, he will not see many faces of color. Indeed, as I was writing this book, the great player and role model Torii Hunter of the Minnesota Twins told *USA Today* that every time a game begins, he scans the stands for African American faces and seldom sees more than two—he calls it the "blackout." Perhaps more African American fans will turn out to witness our young man as he begins his major league career, essentially a Jackie Robinson situation in reverse. The reality is the African American fans are just as much of an endangered species as African American players.

Perhaps our young man picked up a library copy of Jackie Robinson's autobiography, *I Never Had It Made,* and read this paragraph:

> I thought I had learned the worst there was to learn about racial hatred in America. The year 1949 taught me more. A black man, even after he has proven himself on and off the playing field, will still be denied his rights. I am not talking about the things that happened to me in order to portray myself as some kind of martyr. I am recording them because I want to warn the white world that young blacks today are not willing—nor should they be—to enjoy the humiliations I did.[*]

Or perhaps our young friend read all the way through to the epilogue of Robinson's autobiography and found these words:

> I know that I haven't got the right to say truthfully that I have it made. I cannot possibly believe I have it made while so many of my black brothers and sisters are hungry, inadequately housed, insufficiently clothed, denied their dignity as they live in slums or barely exist on welfare. I cannot say I have it made when our country drives full speed ahead to deeper rifts between men and

[*] Robinson, Jackie, *I Never Had It Made, An Autobiography As Told to Alfred Duckett,* G. P. Putnam's Sons, New York, 1972, p. 88.

women of varying colors, speeds along a course toward more and more racism.[*]

If so, our young man might recognize, once he enters the major leagues, that he is bookended with the individual who sacrificed so much, but whose efforts are now receding into the past.

[*] Robinson, *I Never Had It Made,* p. 277.

CHAPTER 5

The Players

We live in an era of exposés, black-eyed brawls, and scandals, and the question of steroids and other so-called performance-enhancing substances is one of the worst scandals to hit Major League Baseball, or any sport, perhaps since the White Sox threw the World Series. The response of many in baseball is practical: "Steroids cannot make a bad player good, they can only make a good player a little bit better," and therefore it's not that big a deal. However, drugs are illegal, and they cause physical harm to the athletes that use them. Few would dispute what the presence of a leader or champion of a sport does for increased youth participation and fan, media, and team community following. This is evidenced in sports like golf with Tiger Woods, or tennis with the Williams sisters. And if role-model athletes at the top are using these drugs, then every athlete under them, down to kids in their teenage years, feels he has to use them to be great.

There are two problems with the initial (official) reaction of the Players Association to the steroid problem. The first is they turned a blind eye to its existence, and then, in vehemently protecting the players' "rights to privacy," they created a sense of defensiveness so great that fans are only left to assume that players in large numbers are abusing performance-enhancing drugs. I'm pleased the issue was forced to be addressed head-on, and that

now there are stringent penalties in place for drug use. Until baseball got its act together regarding its approach to drugs, why should baseball fans have done anything but scorn the game they once loved?

Baseball is a game not just of performance but also of statistics, legends, and lore. If steroids and other drugs are tampering with baseball's beloved statistics and its legends, then a good part of our fan base will surely melt away. Baseball players and the industry are both role models and major influences in the behavior and lifestyle of so many young people. The game has been forced to clean itself up; I know the fallout and the feelings of people regarding these changes. Yet the relationship between players and fans involves much more than resolving the drug issue.

When I was coming up in MLB, you couldn't help but have close contact with the fans. Inside and outside of the ballpark, players and fans parked in the same parking lot and rode the same elevators and escalators. The fans showed up early to watch players take batting and infield practice. Today, for reasons of security *and* convenience, players are carefully protected from the fans, parking in separate guarded lots, accessing the stadium through entrances unreachable to the average fan, and not even reappearing after batting practice in front of the fans for infield practice. In years gone by, baseball players, whose salaries were often not enough to cover their yearly living expenses, would make frequent paid and unpaid appearances in local schools, churches, temples, and other venues, cementing relationships between themselves and their fans; and they worked jobs in the off-season to make ends meet.

Today, you rarely see players where they live. They fly in private jets and play private golf, so it is unlikely that your paths will frequently cross. The only place a fan can get "up close and personal" with a player is at a baseball card or memorabilia show, where the fan has to buy his way in and then present an item to be autographed. And yet, even the autograph has become more imper-

sonal because of the memorabilia market. The quest for autographs from fans is interpreted by players as a means of making money off them, not because they adore the player as a person. Players are stalked at the park, at hotels and airports, at restaurants, and they feel duped when they find these same people sending over an innocent child or a pretty girl to ask for that moneymaking autograph.

On the other hand, some ballplayers don't even look up to acknowledge the fans in the ballpark—many of whom are children—who have paid money and waited in line just for a moment in their presence. The changes have brought on a new view of the players in fans' eyes. They are no longer perceived as being friendly, caring, or accessible. The general belief that all ballplayers are paid a lot of money also makes them seem more alien to the average fan. They make so much they certainly don't live close to or associate with the fans today. Again, money changes perceptions and creates a distance that wasn't always a part of the equation. Plus, with the strikes, lockouts, and work stoppages, players have been viewed as not caring about the fans and the game, concerned only about an amount of money that is more than most fans will earn in a lifetime.

Clearly, the players need to go a long way toward reestablishing the close bonds that used to exist between them and their fans. I've already seen efforts through the Players Trust—the charitable arm of the Players Association. But it's time for the players to get even more guidance from the Players Association about how to relate to the fans. The players are trying to come out of hiding to be role models, community leaders, and more fan-friendly. The fact is it won't happen fast enough or on the scale needed until there is agreement between MLB and the MLBPA, and a working relationship and combined effort toward projects that affect the public and youth to ameliorate this situation.

Wherever I go, from the airport to the gym to restaurants to the movie theater, I have the privilege of meeting people who tell me,

"Dave, I met you twenty years ago at such and such, and you were very gracious to my son." Or, "We met at a 'Turn It Around!' antidrug meeting that you conducted, and you gave me an autograph and we spoke for a couple of minutes. It was a great moment for me." I've always tried to treat the public with respect because that is who I am—after all, they are the ones who ultimately pay our salaries and make our wonderful lives possible. So today, you could say that I reap the benefits of the goodwill that I tried to establish not just for myself but for the game of baseball, ten or twenty or twenty-five years ago.

Unfortunately, today's players won't have nearly as many of those experiences. The players are not getting to touch lives the way we did. Modern players' lives would be much more fulfilling—not in a material sense, but in a personal or even spiritual sense—if they had more contact with the fans. I'm not talking about situations where ten-year-old boys come up to you with half a dozen baseballs in fishnet bags attached to their belts, where they're commanding you to sign each ball right on the sweet spot, so they can maximize its value on eBay! People who just want an autograph on something they can sell on eBay are easy to spot. You can see them coming a mile away. I wish we could spot terrorists as easily as we can identify those professional autograph hounds!

I'm not talking about those kinds of contacts. I'm talking about the genuine one-on-one moments or group meetings where individuals get to express to you what you've meant to them as an athlete, a community member, and a role model. These are extraordinary moments. I wouldn't trade any of these encounters for a million dollars. Today's players already have the millions of dollars. It would be great if they could get out there and experience more of those priceless moments.

But before we get too deeply into the question of the role of the players in Baseball United, let's ask a very simple and important question:

Who wouldn't want to be a Major League Baseball player?

It's the dream of practically every young person to excel in sports, to be the best at every level of competition, to climb the talent ladder all the way to the very top, to reach the major leagues. And why not? Almost everybody else has to commute to work, to nine-to-five jobs they may or may not enjoy. Although it's hard work, the major league ballplayer gets to play a game for a living—and these days, it's a highly lucrative living. You're in the public eye, you've got the adulation and the glory, and you have the chance to prove yourself day after day against the best athletes and competitors in the world. Look at the back of every uniform: What better way to make a name for yourself?

The perks aren't bad, either. Six weeks of spring training in Florida or Arizona isn't so hard to take. Neither is the first-class and private air travel. Everybody wants to be your friend and all the ladies want to get to know you better. You're on the inside, part of the team, sharing a bond with your fellow players as you seek to reach your personal and team goals—a World Series ring, a Most Valuable Player award, a Gold Glove, the Hall of Fame. Make a space for yourself in sports and American history.

And we have to take a moment to talk about the money. The minimum salary for a major league ballplayer is $384,000, and the average major league ballplayer today earns close to $2.8 million. Top ballplayers earn $10 million to $24 million. That's something like $100,000 a game for a player like Derek Jeter or Barry Bonds, with the best benefits and pension of any industry in the world for its members. Not a bad way to establish your financial future and the financial security of your family.

When baseball salaries first hit a million dollars, Bob Ryan, a sports columnist for the *Boston Globe,* wrote that it was unconscionable for parents to tell their kids to quit playing baseball and come inside and do their homework!

Of course, for all the millions of individuals who might wish to don a Major League Baseball uniform, only a few will ever make it to the big leagues. That's why baseball players (and all professional athletes) are so important in society. They encapsulate our hopes and dreams—for ourselves, and for our children. For every Major League Baseball player, there are millions of individuals gazing at that player and wondering what it must be like to have the privilege of putting on that uniform every day. It must be the greatest thing in the world.

It is. I won't lie. I loved being a Major League Baseball player. I loved the challenge of it. I especially loved the fact that baseball is the most cerebral of all sports, that it requires the most conscious thought, that it takes the longest to master because of its many intricacies, complexities, and subtleties. The fact that if you can hit major league pitching, you are in a very small class of athletes. It's great to be part of the elite, and I'm very fortunate to have won seven Gold Glove awards, six Silver Slugger awards, to have 3,110 base hits and 1,833 RBI, to have stolen a couple hundred bases, to have won the World Series, and to have made a lot of friends in and around the game across the country and across our borders, and after retirement, to have received the ultimate accolade of going to the Baseball Hall of Fame.

When I was playing for the Yankees, Mario Cuomo was elected governor of the state of New York. It was the pinnacle of his political career, and yet, when they asked him how it felt to be elected governor in a very tough race, he immediately responded, "It's great, but I would much rather be the starting center fielder for the New York Yankees."

Sorry, Mario. I know it's very difficult to become governor of a state, and you covered the governor's mansion in New York with great range and agility. But even you couldn't have mastered what it takes to cover the territory that Mickey Mantle, Bernie Williams, and even on occasion yours truly, had the privilege to patrol. In short, everybody wants to be a major leaguer. I know for a fact our present president, George W. Bush, would have loved to have a baseball career on his résumé—well, baseball club owner and president of the United States isn't so bad, either. Bush also settles for hosting T-ball on the White House lawn each year—part of his contribution of giving back to the game.

Given the fact that there are so many amazing aspects to a Major League Baseball career, it can sound downright churlish and even hypocritical for ballplayers to complain about how difficult their lives really are. But let's take a moment and look realistically at the life of a Major League Baseball player. Set aside for a moment the money, the adulation, the perks, and the ability to play a game for a living. I'd like to share with you a fuller picture of the pressures that Major League Baseball players face, so that you can get a broader understanding of what their lives are like and of the challenges they face if they are to play a meaningful role in Baseball United.

Let's talk about job security for a moment. Whatever you do for a living, there are tens of thousands who want your job and are convinced that they can do it better than you. In our society, though, many protections exist to keep individuals secure in their jobs. Civil servants and teachers have tenure, lawyers become partners, and business executives often receive "golden parachutes" (also known as "golden handcuffs") that protect them financially in the event that the company decides to let them go.

Major League Baseball players have different job protection, otherwise known as the Players Association. There's always somebody younger, faster, more agile, a better hitter, and more competitive, gunning for your job. In fact, there are a lot of those people. Some of them are teammates with whom you play, eat, live, and travel for seven or eight months of the year. Others are competitors you face at the major league level. Still others are the "bonus babies" working their way up through the minors, staking their careers on getting that lucky break that catapults them into your job. Once your eyesight and mobility give out on you—or, God forbid, back-to-back "off" years or an injury confronts you—you're out. There are very few fields as competitive as professional sports.

Second, as a baseball player, your most important asset is your body. Yet the human body simply wasn't meant to endure the punishment of playing as many as two hundred games—if you add in spring training and postseason games—in a season. A career-limiting or career-ending injury can occur at any moment in a collision with another player, while training, on the base paths, even getting hit by a pitch. Very few professions require you to put your most valuable asset—your own body—in harm's way on a more constant basis than baseball. That's why players get so quiet when one of their own is taken off the field after an injury. Certainly we're thinking about our brother athlete, but you'd better believe we're also thinking about ourselves.

In addition to the physical strain that baseball places on the athlete's body, major leaguers also have to contend with the emotional strain of playing a game in which failure is a constant. We all admire the .300 hitter, but that batting average implies a failure rate of seven out of ten times. Not only that, you are failing seven out of ten trips to the plate in the most conspicuous, public manner imaginable. When most people make a mistake at work, they don't have forty or fifty thousand people laughing and booing at them or feeling genuine disappointment, children included. They certainly don't have those mistakes replayed on television or reported in the newspaper. They say that players who are overly affected by fan criticism have thin skin or "rabbit ears." But you've got to develop a pretty thick skin—and a pretty tough psyche—to contend not just with the external criticism from the fans but that voice within you that says, "You're a failure. You're never gonna hit that pitcher. You're in a slump. You've lost the touch. They're going to bench you, they're going to send you to the minors, they're going to release you." New York Yankee Alex Rodriguez is the most visible example of the challenges of this negative criticism. You wouldn't wish this on anyone.

That's just at the plate. In the field, your team expects practically nothing less than perfection. When you make an error, especially a mental error, you know you're letting your teammates down. But you're also letting your fans down, and they're going to let you know it in the most vociferous manner possible. By comparison, seldom do corporate executives get public reprimands. Microsoft typically releases software that contains tens or even hundreds of thousands of bugs or shortcomings that will be corrected down the road. While Microsoft has plenty of critics, they don't all gather at Safeco Field in Seattle in groups of fifty thousand to boo, snicker, and point at Bill Gates in center field. In other words, most people get to make their mistakes in private, and their careers are not defined by those mistakes.

Look back at baseball in the twentieth century. If you are old enough to remember 1986, and if I say the name Bill Buckner, what comes to mind? An outstanding career as a hitter, fielder, and team leader? A great teammate and a truly game ballplayer? Or that ball trickling through his legs in game six of the 1986 World Series with the Mets?

Or think about Carlos Beltran, in the pouring rain at Shea Stadium, in the bottom of the ninth, bases loaded, his Mets down by two, in the seventh game of the 2006 National League Championship Series. His career, unfortunately, may be forever defined by the sight of his bat frozen to his shoulder with that seventy-six-mile-an-hour change-up turning into a called strike three.

If you go back further, there's the famous "third strike drop" in the 1941 World Series, when Brooklyn Dodgers catcher Mickey Owen inadvertently kicked what would have been strike three into the opposing Yankees' dugout, prolonging the inning and ultimately costing the Dodgers the World Series. And if you want to go back almost a hundred years, there's Fred Merkle of the Chicago Cubs, whose great career as a Major League Baseball player was permanently overshadowed by one error, commonly referred to as "Merkle's Boner." The only reason die-hard baseball fans remember Fred Merkle, a century after he played, isn't because he played the game well. It's because he made one mistake that will live on forever.

So every time you step onto the field, they may be paying you a lot of money, and there may be pretty girls or scores of messages from "friends" waiting for you at the team hotel. But you've got a lot more opponents than just the guys in the other dugout. You've got your own psychology to manage, as you deal with the repeated failure that even the best baseball players endure. You've got the instant feedback from a stadium full of people who may harbor envy and resentment toward you if you're making a good major league salary and not producing to their expectations. You've got the constant threat of injury, you've got the concern that other players are looking to take away your job, and we haven't even begun to talk about the media.

One of the biggest changes in the landscape of baseball since I began playing professionally in 1973 has been the rise of media, with sports talk radio, cable TV sports networks like ESPN and Fox Sports Net, sports panel shows, and, of course, the ubiquitous Internet. When I was playing baseball, especially in the 1970s with the Padres, CNN was just a gleam in the eye of Ted Turner and ESPN was probably nothing more than a business plan in the briefcase of a guy named Bill Rasmussen. Back then, even after I'd been in the league for a few years, when the Padres came into a city like Pittsburgh, people wouldn't even know who I was. They'd see that I was big and athletic-looking, so they'd say to me, "Are you an athlete? Who are you? Do you play football? Basketball?" They were always surprised to find out that I was a baseball player and a member of the San Diego Padres! Back then, many of the best baseball players were simply unknown outside their home cities.

Imagine a Barry Bonds or a David Ortiz walking through an airport today and having people come up to him and saying, "What sport do you play?" They've seen his first hit, and his latest, greatest play, and probably know a slew of personal data—

where he lives and how much money he makes—especially if he's recently been accused of something scandalous. Privacy is gone—while on the flip side of the coin, fame can be immediate, if not premature.

When I first started playing, if you wanted to read about baseball, you looked at your daily newspaper and you got a story about the game and you got the box score. West Coast games didn't appear in the East Coast papers the next morning. If you lived in the East and a late game was played on the West Coast, you'd have to turn on the radio to find out who won. If you wanted more in-depth coverage, you'd wait for your copy of *Sports Illustrated* to arrive in the mail. It was a simpler time, and to be frank, it was an easier time for ballplayers.

Today, if you make any kind of mistake, on or off the field, it's going to be immediately amplified throughout the media, dissected on dozens of TV and radio sports talk shows and panel discussion shows, shown endlessly on the myriad sports TV news shows, and preserved for all time on the Internet. Opinions sprout everywhere. There's no place to hide. Half a century ago, reporters traveled with the teams and kept the secrets. They knew that young people wanted to look up to ballplayers and they would keep players' foibles—their propensity to drink, gamble, or womanize—out of the newspapers. Few people knew about Babe Ruth's propensities, and even fewer cared. He meant so much to people in a positive way that nobody pried into his personal life or tried to exploit his reputation for an exposé.

Back then, the press (this was way before we started calling it the "media") felt the same responsibility to protect baseball that they did to protect a national leader like President Franklin D. Roosevelt. They never mentioned his polio in news reports, nor did they show him displaying any physical infirmity, such as when he would be placed in or moved from his wheelchair. The reporters felt compelled to present an image of the president as strong, forceful, and powerful, so they chose not to report on any aspect of his life that might compromise that projection of strength. Similarly, they protected the game of baseball by keeping the ballplayers' private business exactly that—private.

Of course, we live in a different age. I'm certainly not advocating a return to the 1940s or 1950s, when reporters typically saw themselves as baseball's partners and not baseball's adversaries. But today, the media circus that surrounds baseball and every professional sport can often be a distraction for players while adding little "new news" or even information of substance to the public. Players are hesitant to get too close to members of the media because of its insatiable hunger for information.

Fans are subjected to a daily barrage of seemingly mild-mannered sports writers shouting at each other about every issue and nonissue, no matter how trivial. Is it good television? It gets ratings. Is it edifying? Sometimes. Can you watch those shows and come away with a greater knowledge of the game, its nuances, or the personalities of its players? Yes, but at what cost? The new media that surrounds baseball serves as a giant echo chamber, radiating into the world of the sports fan a constant din of noise.

In my day, many players would maintain that they "didn't read the newspapers." I think many more players offered that denial than actually lived by it. Players naturally wanted to know what was being written about them. But today, it's just not possible for a ballplayer to create a cocoon around himself where he is not conscious of the media's constant glare. Today, a player might make one mistake early in his career, and that mistake will be broadcast and rebroadcast and repeated endlessly throughout the new media echo chamber, tainting or even destroying that player's career or reputation even before he has had a chance to establish himself on the field.

For example, as I write, there is a news story on the Internet about a particular minor league prospect who threw a bat at an umpire after a called strike three. This young man, whose name

I will not mention because I don't want to add to his problems—and I know he's recognized his mistake and wishes he could take back that moment in time—could have turned on his laptop this morning, gone to Google News, and instantly discovered that his mishap with the umpire—a moment of youthful frustration—was available to be dissected by an international audience of sports fans in 166 news outlets, from New York to Aberdeen, Scotland, to Macon, Georgia, to Tokyo. You can be sure that the video clip will follow him forever, a scarlet letter and a defining moment for this twenty-one-year-old athlete who, until that moment, had been touted as one of the best minor league prospects in the game.

We all know of certain famous ballplayers who will either not speak to the media, or who will grant interviews only rarely and on very specific, guarded terms, while other ball players are almost unbridled when they talk to the media. They want popularity, they want their name out there, and they possess a burning desire to catapult their fame with off-field endorsement opportunities.

Yes, media is a sharp, double-edged sword. But I think you can understand why the level of trust that once existed between ballplayers and the sports and news media has been all but destroyed. Sports news is as competitive as the sports themselves. The pressure to get a scoop, accurate or otherwise, is so intense that ballplayers tend to look at the media as bottom feeders, waiting to pounce on them for the slightest mistake, misstep, or miscue with no compunction or remorse. Yes, baseball players have it great, but at the same time, they live under the harsh, unforgiving, relentless, and often magnified glare of the media, in every moment of their professional and personal lives, in and off season.

There is also another unexpected phenomenon related to *Sports-Center*. When I was playing ball in New York, the epitome of a great moment at Yankee Stadium was that you might hear WCBS-TV Channel 2's sports announcer, the highly enthusiastic Warner Wolf, talking about a home run you hit or a great play you made in the field and shouting his trademark "Let's go to the videotape!" Well, we've moved away from videotape, and we've entered the digital era. Now with *SportsCenter* compiling highlights of every game into a single hour show, every athlete hopes to see himself on *SportsCenter* in the "Top Ten Plays of the Day." The athlete knows that all of his peers are watching, and so is every sports fan. Sometimes you get the sense that players are more interested in media exposure than they are in winning games.

What makes it onto *SportsCenter*? Anything that the most casual sports fan would find visually appealing—the three-run bomb, the catch where the fielder tumbles into the stands, the collision at home plate. What doesn't make it onto *SportsCenter*? Any of the intricacies that make baseball the great game it is: hitting behind the runner to move him over and put him in scoring position, hitting the cutoff man and preventing a runner from advancing into scoring position, laying down a bunt or sacrificing yourself for the team.

Times have changed. If you want to be famous today as a ballplayer, you're not necessarily thinking about doing the things that help out your team. You're thinking about doing the things that are going to get you adulation, exposure, a big contract or a spot on the highlight reel. *SportsCenter, Baseball Tonight,* and even www.MLB.com certainly capture the most dramatic and exciting moments of baseball, but by putting a premium on those events, they ignore the nuances that make the game great.

In addition, the media often becomes the pawn of the team owners when contract negotiation time looms for a player, even a star or a fan favorite. It works this way: A player's agent will make a case for his client's salary by comparing the player statistically to other players at that position throughout the league. If the player's statistics are similar to higher paid players at that same position on other teams, the agent can make a compelling argument, either in negotiations or in arbitration, that his player is worth at least as much.

So as to diminish the value of a baseball player, owners will frequently begin a campaign of criticism against a player who is up for arbitration, free agency, or simply at the end of his contract period. Owners will often tell favored media writers that a ballplayer is lazy, won't play hurt, is not a team player, only gets his base hits—or for a pitcher, strikeouts—during "garbage time" when games have become all but impossible to win or lose, and so on. There is no end to the negative comments that owners can and will make about players whose financial futures are on the line. It's practically impossible for a player to counter the negativity that owners spew forth. And with so many news outlets on cable TV, in talk radio, and online, it's never been so easy for management to trash one of its ballplayers.

I'm not looking for sympathy for multimillionaires. I share this with you because I want you to understand the real life of ballplayers, the emotional struggles they face and the psychological battles they endure every day. While it has never been more rewarding financially to be a ballplayer, it's never been harder to survive as a ballplayer, given the full range of pressure brought down on them every day. Stress and exposure have made them more insular and have changed the relationship between players and the media, fans, and community.

It's against this backdrop that players will consider whether or not they want to participate in a program like Baseball United. You can understand their reticence and reluctance. We are asking people who bear the burdens of celebrities to become more deeply involved in their communities, to cooperate with the media and ownership when all of these elements seem to conspire to beat them down. I just want to say that, ballplayers, I feel your pain. I've been there. But you are truly blessed. Take the time to give back.

I certainly endured my share of suspicion when I was seeking to contribute to the community early in my career with the Padres and then later on with the Yankees. It took people ten years to believe that the Winfield Foundation, and my concern for the community, was sincere. When I began the practice of donating large amounts of Padres tickets to organizations that worked with underprivileged youth, the most common response was not "What a great guy Dave is!" It was "What's the angle? Why is he doing this? Is this a tax scam? What's he getting out of it?" We're talking about a level of suspicion that approached outright paranoia, and this was in mellow San Diego, back in the relatively innocent 1970s!

Fast-forward ten years to my time with the New York Yankees. By then, it had become more common for players to establish their own foundations and give back some of their sudden wealth to the communities where they played or where they came from. Sports agents like Leigh Steinberg demanded that his clients contribute to the community and not just stick everything in the bank (or spend it all, for that matter). But in the early 1980s, you could barely pick up one of the tabloid newspapers in New York without finding more criticism and suspicion from Yankee ownership about the Winfield Foundation. Again, my motives were considered suspect and people questioned my "loyalty" to the team and to the game.

In the early part of my career, well-known ballplayers tended to stay in one place for several years, if not for an entire career. I played the bulk of my career with two teams—the Padres and the Yankees, and then had relatively brief stints with the Angels, the Blue Jays, the Twins, and the Indians. In my era, though, you still had the George Bretts, Kirby Pucketts, Cal Ripkens, Jim Rices, Jim Palmers, and Tony Gwynns, superstars who played for one team throughout their careers. That's how it was in the days before free agency, when a team essentially owned you for life.

Today, things are very different, of course. The era of free agency has ushered in a period in which players usually spend a much shorter amount of time in any given city with any given team. As a result, it's harder for players to establish an identity or a loyal following for themselves in the community. They know they may not be there very long, and the fans know it, too.

Connection to the fans is important. Fans know that baseball is a business, but it's a unique kind of business, a game in which the fans (also paying customers) feel not just a personal connection but a sense of ownership. People feel attached to sports in a way that they don't feel attached to other major entities in society. No one ever says, "Oh, IBM, I'll remember you forever! That laptop I bought in 1986—I'll never forget it!" Or, "Hitachi, I'll never forget that wonderful TV I bought from you back in 1993—I was sorry to see it retire." We don't feel attached to major corporations offering goods and services we use every day, but we feel attached to our teams.

It's tough for fans when a favorite player moves to another team, especially to a hated rival, as in the case of Johnny Damon moving from the Red Sox to the Yankees, or Tom Glavine moving from the Braves to the Mets. Players moving around more often and staying for briefer periods of time means that the connection between players and fans is diminished. It's difficult to stay connected to an individual player when you know there's a chance that player will be playing for another team next year, or—sometimes worse—when a player stays with a team for many years, but then finishes his career elsewhere. This makes it difficult for ballplayers who are committed to giving back to the community, simply because they don't know if they'll *be* back next year, or even next week.

When players, teams, and Major League Baseball actually engage in community service, there is still no system in place to publicize these efforts. The public tends not to pay attention because there is no meaningful common cause and because there is no connected relationship or action between MLB and the players.

Baseball is especially weak in this area in comparison with pro football and pro basketball. The NBA and NFL have their acts together when it comes to publicizing the good works that their players do. It's impossible to watch an NFL or NBA game without seeing messages from their respective leagues showing ballplayers interacting with kids at an event sponsored by United Way, a library association, or some similar charitable group. They've been proactive, consistent, and highly visible for years. When there is a national disaster, the NBA and the NFL are quick to act, and equally quick to publicize their actions.

I am speaking not just of what the leagues do as a whole, but also the personal efforts of individual players. For example, after Hurricane Katrina, a group of NBA stars called each other on the phone and set up a charity game in Atlanta, with all the proceeds, including five-figure donations from each player, to go toward Hurricane Katrina relief. MLB and the players gave $10 million toward Katrina relief, and they did the same for relief funds after 9/11—but you probably never heard of either contribution. The NFL and the NBA have extremely savvy public relations teams who made sure that fans knew about those charitable endeavors even though they weren't official league charity events.

Did you even know the Players Association has a charitable trust? Did news of that donation last more than a single news cycle? Baseball has a lot to learn from other sports when it comes to creating awareness of the fact that its players give back to the same degree or greater than those in other sports.

Earlier, I mentioned the difficulties I faced when I was seeking to establish the David M. Winfield Foundation, first in San Diego and then in New York. Today, by contrast, it's incredibly easy for a ballplayer to establish his own foundation. They no longer have to rent office space, hire attorneys, bring in staff, and do all the things that a typical foundation has to do. Instead, through the Major League Baseball Players Trust, they can go to the MLBPA website's Players Trust page (http://mlbplayers.mlb .com/NASApp/mlb/pa/trust/about.jsp), click their mouse a few times, and instantly a foundation is established in their names. All they have to do is write the check, and contributions can be managed and directed by the managers of the foundation.

I certainly understand and respect the choice that some ballplayers make, as do many other citizens, to keep their charitable and financial donations private. My opinion is that this is not a time for baseball to be modest. When the game is tainted by steroids, strikes, and other controversies, lurching from crisis to crisis, baseball needs all the good ink it can get. And baseball will not be able to establish links to the community until there is a strong working relationship between MLB and the players. The two camps need to first work with each other.

Until there is a change, I urge players like Derek Jeter, Torii Hunter, and the scores of others to be more public about their community involvement. I also urge the fans to recognize the fact that even though a baseball player today may not be in a particular city for his entire career, he is trying, in the space of time available as a member of that community, to do something special for the kids, for those in hospitals, for those in the inner city, for whatever charitable endeavor with which he seeks to involve himself.

It's great to be a Major League Baseball player, as I said at the start of this chapter. But it's important for the players to do more, and it's equally important for owners to quit using the media as a means of degrading players and destroying their reputations in the eyes of their fans. Baseball players have to overcome the negativity they almost certainly feel toward the fishbowl environment in which they live, and make themselves more available to their communities, and the fans have to respect just how much they are giving.

It's hard to pick up a newspaper without reading about some city spending hundreds of millions of dollars on a shiny new ballpark. Now it's New York's turn, as the city will be home to not just one, but two new ballparks, costing close to two billion dollars, if everything goes as planned (and that's not always how things work in New York—trust me!). I've seen the plans for the new Yankee Stadium, and they are preparing to scrap Shea as well. Both organizations will set a new standard for respecting the old tradition and history of the ballpark, while incorporating the new. But the real assets of baseball are not the stadiums, or the luxury boxes, or the jerseys, or even the international markets where they are selling more and more apparel and souvenirs.

The chief asset of baseball is its players. They literally and figuratively are the face of the game—its charisma, personality, and character. They are the source of connection between the game and the fans. They give the game its rich history. Baseball needs to publicize these remarkable individuals in a more effective way, so that the sporting world learns more, and not just about the negative events that get amplified over the Internet and sports talk radio, and on the "shouting match" sports news TV programs. Baseball fans and society at large need to know more about the greatness of the players and their accomplishments, both on and off the field. It won't happen without the plan and vision of Baseball United.

CHAPTER 6

The Agents

Maybe it was the movie *Jerry Maguire.* Maybe it's the public's disgust with high player salaries. Whatever the reason, sports agents are some of the most unpopular people in the world of professional sports. In that world, agents probably rank just above scalpers in terms of how little they are admired by the public. Yet with the money top agents make, they could care less about their public image and they just do their job.

The image the media projects of sports agents isn't favorable. They are often portrayed as brazen, self-centered, smug power brokers, zipping around in expensive sports cars while talking incessantly on cell phones. They make outrageous deals for players that only contribute to the exorbitant—and rising—cost of the services of their flamboyant clients, which in turn adds to the cost of taking a family to a game. There has been an evolution of the agent in the past thirty-five years. Initially, they didn't even have to be licensed. Today they are, and in order to obtain that license there are fees, an application, and a highly scrutinizing approval process.

The belittling of their character is unfair. Without an agent's involvement, most players could not navigate the complexities of today's contracts. Certainly, many of the most successful agents are demanding, hard-nosed, and arrogant. But to a certain degree, they have to be, given that they are going up against the lords of baseball—the owners—men who did not make it to the top because they were weak businessmen. A baseball player has the opportunity to negotiate a contract very few times in his career, and the owners provide stiff opposition when players make their salary demands, sometimes, as I discussed, even going so far as to use the media against them.

Players may complain about ownership, but for the most part, they don't. They recognize that when it comes to influencing the media and shaping the public's perception of a ballplayer, the owners have the upper hand.

The agent's job is not nearly as simple as many people think—they don't just sit down with an owner over a beer, ask for ten million, hear the owner offer six, and then split the difference. Their world is as hypercompetitive as that of the players they represent. Just as an athlete is often viewed as being only as good as the last game he played, agents are judged by the same scale: They're only as good as the last deal they closed. Their successes and failures occur in the harsh glare of the media spotlight, just like those of their clients.

A big win means increased interest in their firm on the part of top players, prospects, and their families. Failure to show the client the money, the overused *Jerry Maguire* phrase, means that new clients are likely to shy away from their firm, and even their current clients may be wooed away by aggressive competitors.

Some agents wield considerable power, although often the perception of their power is greater than the reality. This suits the agents fine, because in their world, perception often *is* reality. In the real world, no agent—no matter how famous or successful, no matter how powerful his client roster—has magical powers over general managers even though the media might speculate that this is the case. The function agents perform is so vital because a player's career is brief, and can end even sooner due to injury.

Sometimes I wonder whether some of the agents actually

advise their clients to be outrageous, so as to create curiosity on the part of the fans. I call it the "Rodman factor." The more you're like Dennis Rodman, or more recently, Terrell Owens, the more ink you'll get in the newspaper. I don't necessarily think that's good for baseball. There's a certain dignity with which the best players carry themselves, on and off the field—a Derek Jeter, a Trevor Hoffman, an Orel Hersheiser, and, some might say, a Dave Winfield.

It used to be that agents and general managers would talk about batting average, win-loss records, or ERA when debating contracts. Today, agents, as well as teams, come up with complex computer models that run hundreds of pages long, with statistical analysis comparing one player with all others at his position or in his category. These models can cost thousands of dollars to research and prepare and turn the wonderful sport of baseball into arcane number-crunching. Of course, if I were playing today, I'd have my agents create one of those things for me, too! It's funny to think about how one player in 2006 can "lose" at arbitration . . . and still walk away with a ten-million-dollar annual salary. Now that's my idea of losing!

Before I turn to the subject of how agents can play a role in Baseball United, it's worth taking a brief look back at baseball history to see how the owner-player negotiation dance has evolved over the decades.

Until the 1970s, players were rarely permitted to have agents, but agents were hardly needed in the first place. Typically, a ballplayer would complete his season and then go home, where he invariably worked a second job just to make ends meet—baseball was never the most lucrative of professions, except for the top stars. At some point over the winter, a letter from the owner of the team would arrive in the mail, complete with contract. Occasionally, there was a marginal raise in admiration of his spunkiness, but there was no negotiating. The player's only options were to accept the owner's offered salary, accept a trade, or retire then and there. Because of the reserve clause, there was no such thing as free agency, meaning that a team essentially owned the rights of a player for the entirety of his career. The owners had all the power and the players had none.

If the player did not receive his contract or did not mail it back signed, then the classic scene of the face-to-face meeting in the owner's office would take place. (I caught the brunt of one of those exchanges early in my career and was advised from afar, "Take the two-thousand-dollar raise or go drive a truck!") The owner enjoyed total power in an office meeting. You had a ballplayer, often with little education and certainly no business experience, knocking timidly on the door of a baronial, luxurious office suite. Instead of mailing the player the contract, the owner would hand it over in person, thus informing the player exactly how much money he was going to make in the upcoming season. The player was not permitted to bring anyone with him into that meeting—no agent, no attorney, nobody.

The player, no matter how good his year might have been, would inevitably be intimidated in such splendid surroundings. His choices were the same as if he had received the contract in the mail back home: sign, be traded, or retire. There was no such thing as real negotiating, and there was no such thing as holding out.

In 1970, when Jim Bouton published the seminal baseball book *Ball Four,* he wrote that in the 1960s, a player would have considered it almost unthinkable to tell anyone else on the team how much he was making. Ballplayers knew nothing of what their teammates and competitors were earning. It became increasingly clear that if players were going to get a fair piece of the revenues they were generating through their on-field actions, they would need some serious help.

By the early 1970s, baseball players realized they needed their own representation, bringing about the rise of agents. Though, of course, owners strongly resisted the idea that players should have knowledgeable assistance and experienced negotiators at their side. When players' agents first came on the scene, the sound they had to get used to was not that of a cash register ringing, but the click of the telephone being hung up on them.

The owners didn't respect the agents, and initially no one responded to them. The same applied to the fledgling Players Association: If you wanted to be your team's player representative, your career could very well be in jeopardy, particularly if you were not a strong or extraordinary player. The first brave souls to provide guidance as agents had to build a clientele on success. The agencies themselves were initially run on a mom-and-pop basis; they were not the well-oiled machines that they are today, and the entire sports agent field was unregulated.

As time passed, the Major League Baseball Players Association began to regulate agents and instituted a certification process. Today, we have moved from the era of the mom-and-pop agent to that of the super sports conglomerate, such as SFX, Assante, Clear Channel, and Beverly Hills Sports Council, along with major individual agents such as the respected and disliked (for his hard-nosed, salary-escalating tactics and successes) Scott Boras, the Hendricks brothers, and Jeffrey Morrad, who was often described as the "real-life Jerry Maguire," until he crossed over and became part of the Arizona Diamondbacks' management group.

The phenomenon of the player's agent, combined with free agency and arbitration, makes it possible for players to secure a large salary upon entry into the league (in 2007, a minimum of $384,000), and to receive what they can through player comparisons. Today, players feel entitled to reach their free-agency year, weigh their options, entertain offers, and move wherever the money and other terms are best. As a player, I agree that this makes the most sense.

I don't want to give the impression that these guys are angels, however. The business has gotten increasingly cutthroat in recent years. Some agents are grabbing kids and talking to them while they're still in high school and college, disrespecting the NCAA rules. These agents, or individuals working on their behalf, are establishing relationships with budding athletes and their families, getting them tickets for events, doing favors, arranging jobs—just as in other sports. This is neither legal nor proper, and yet it happens all the time.

Additionally, agents are flexing their power in ways that are potentially detrimental to the game. Some agents are bold enough to complain about matters ranging from pitch count to playing time for their clients, virtually all of whom have contracts tied to incentives, incentives which require the player to be out on the field in order to reach target numbers. Managers now must worry about issues other than simply winning, just to keep their star players—and those players' agents—happy.

Conflict of interest on multiple levels is also a concern in today's modern world of baseball agents. A potential conflict of interest arises when an agent or agency represents more than one ballplayer at the same position. It may be in the best interests of that agent or agency to make one player look good or bad by comparison with the other when producing a statistical analysis of a player's accomplishments.

These situations are hard to monitor and even harder to resolve. By what legal means can you compel an agency to refrain from taking on another client at the same position? And by what means can you convince a ballplayer that his interests will not be best served by an agency representing another star or potential star who plays the same position that he plays?

The question that concerns me is this: How far will agents go out of their way to be involved in the Baseball United campaign? Is it in their best interest? They understand their job in clear, simple terms: to create the maximum amount of financial security for their clients. Yet sports agents can play an important role in Baseball United by encouraging—or even requiring—their clients to take part in the campaign and find their own unique ways of giving back. Some agents, like Leigh Steinberg, are famous for this practice. Torii Hunter and his agent, Larry Reynolds, are setting standards and manners for giving back as well. What I'd like to see is *all* agents signing on, and guiding and influencing their clients to adopt a sense of responsibility—to the communities from which they hail, to society in general, and to the game that is the wellspring of their financial success. These things are happening on an individual basis across the league, but *everybody* needs to be on board.

When a major storm hits an island in the Caribbean or a region in Latin America from which major league ballplayers come, those players inevitably lead the way in providing financial relief for the victims. They are following, of course, the time-honored example of Roberto Clemente, who organized a relief effort in Puerto Rico after the December 1971 earthquake that leveled Managua, Nicaragua. Clemente boarded a private plane overloaded with relief supplies to make sure that the food and medicine would actually reach the victims. Tragically, Clemente died in the plane crash on that mission of mercy, thus cementing his own place in the baseball firmament and providing a powerful example to those who follow him. The established Roberto Clemente Award now acknowledges players for their work in their communities.

Other ballplayers give back by building stadiums or other baseball facilities in their hometowns, establishing individual foundations or establishing foundations through the Major League Baseball Players Association. Good things are already happening. But what's going on now is only a beginning and has been isolated from a larger cause and purpose.

The agents, because they have the ear of the players in a unique and powerful way, have an opportunity to be leaders in Baseball United because they can speak to even the biggest stars in a way that few others can. The agent should be firm with all of his player-clients, telling them, "This is where Major League Baseball is headed in the twenty-first century, and you've got to get on the bus." Of course, leadership for the campaign cannot come from anywhere but the commissioner, MLB, and the Players Association.

However, agents make up the second tier of leadership that is required for the campaign. I believe agents would get more than a warm fuzzy feeling from serving in a leadership capacity in Baseball United. The media would know which agents are involved and which are not, and agents are aware that any time your name is out there in a positive way, it's good for business. We want to be able to say to the agents, "This is the direction where the game is headed, and you can be among the first to participate."

It's good business for agents, both short-term and long-term. If the game stays healthy, they'll keep making their money. If their player becomes a valuable mainstay for a team and community, even one more year on a contract makes sense. It's easy to be myopic and just focus on the next deal, instead of the more important questions about the future of baseball, but agents, like the rest of us who love the game, must ask these questions.

Agents also have to keep in mind that players do not gain sympathy from the general public when they make increasingly high salary demands, threaten work stoppages, or take positions in collective bargaining with which the American public disagrees, such as on drug testing or other sensitive issues. It's up to the agents to get the players to recognize that there is a golden goose, and it lays eggs in the form of twenty-million-dollar annual salaries—and that goose has to be preserved at all costs!

Agents might read this and say, "Hey, baseball's balance sheet looks great! Everybody's making money! If it ain't broke, don't fix it!" To them, I respond with these questions: Would you say that nothing's wrong with the game of baseball today? Would most people say that? Is the continuing decline in baseball's popularity vis-à-vis other sports an indication of strength or weakness?

You don't wait until an industry falls flat on its face to improve it. Baseball hasn't reached its low point yet. What that nadir may be, and how long it might take to reach it, is anybody's guess. But as long as everyone is focused primarily on short-term gain, the game will get there faster.

I'm calling for the hearts and minds of the agents, for their willing, conspicuous, and constructive participation and involvement in Baseball United. Wouldn't it be great for the game if players said to their agents, "Don't just show me the money. Show some responsibility as a member of this unique, elite group—advisors to major league ballplayers—and show everyone what you can do to make the game stronger."

CHAPTER 7

The Media
and Corporate Partners

It is well understood that the media have changed dramatically in the past forty years. But what is the effect, impact, and purpose of all these sources of "news and views" on baseball today? How far-reaching is this omnipresent component of our sports lives? How many arms does it have? Sports coverage is dictated by the competition for stories (often one-upmanship, in my opinion), for broadcast rights, for the individual media outlets' right to exist, and for their right to lead in a competitive environment. This competition dictates how they act, and not only in a reactive manner: The media have been increasingly proactive and antagonistic in their approach.

Even when it comes to issues vastly more important than sports, such as matters of national security or war propaganda, news and media giants have shown they will forsake security for getting the headlines first.

There is active media (coverage), passive media (distribution of information), tabloids (misinformation), the Internet, talk radio, reality TV—it's truly a *SportsCenter*-addicted generation. People watch and listen to sports twenty-four hours a day, every day of the year. This component of sports today has let the genie out of the bottle. There are no more secrets about athletes. A player's private life or that of his family is no longer out of bounds. The media will shape people's opinions and reactions toward athletes, and all of this has an influence on the way athletes act on the field, in front of a camera, or away from the field altogether. I worked for Fox TV, so I understand both the media and player aspects.

There's no set strategy for players on how to handle the media all the time; a player's image and reputation are constantly being tested. Players cannot simply ask the media to back off, or to give "puff" publicity when it is not warranted. Every media vehicle is a professional organization that has to pay its bills. Even the player with the most integrity can be cast in a poor light by the media.

Regardless, the media are another critical part of any attempt at Baseball United. The media possess the unique power to convince everyone that the campaign is not only real but that it's working, that caring people are involved, and that this campaign and all who are involved are keys to change. You cannot fool or manipulate the media; you cannot buy or bribe them. I understand that the media are not in the business of promoting good works but if the news is good MLB must do everything in its power to make the media aware of it. When baseball begins to reconcile internally, recruit its soldiers, and execute the revitalization plan, the media will have no choice but to cover such a huge industry-changing campaign!

One idea for MLB and all the sports television producers out there: I would love to see a special season-end event in which the top honors in baseball—the Most Valuable Players, the Cy Youngs, the Rookies of the Year, and the Gold Gloves—are presented to the honorees before a live national television audience. It ought to be like the Oscars, glamorous and exciting. Right now, news of these awards emerges in dribs and drabs from MLB. That's not maximizing the publicity value of those

awards and the sports stars who win them. Let's have a
awards night, with season highlights, and former award
and various celebrities making the presentations. Th
be a great way for baseball to showcase its stars to a
audience after the World Series, when interest in baseb
to other sports.

Let's turn now to the subject of advertising. Baseball and
ness world have been partners for over a century. Playe
and leagues enjoy the revenue that comes from corpora
tions, and businesses like the benefits that come from as
themselves with the national pastime. Before baseball ca
packaged with a stick of pink gum, they came inside
packages. No Brooklyn Dodger fan alive can forget the
sign belonging to the men's haberdasher Abe Stark: H
WIN SUIT. I don't know if Stark ever had to give away a si
but the sign is still part of baseball lore.

The chance to be associated with the revitalization of A
national pastime will attract large corporate sponsors, ev
not currently involved with baseball. Many of our grea
tries—automobile manufacturing, steel, or others feelin
competitive pressure—may themselves be in need of a c
renaissance. For these companies, tying into Baseball
would be particularly appropriate.

Or a pharmaceutical company or health food giant mi
to take advantage of its long-standing relationship with tl
and find it effective to link its advertising themes of health
ness to the concept of baseball as a means of uniting gene
I think corporate America will readily understand the b
opportunities associated with the Baseball United camp

One corporate leader in particular stands out. Bank o
ica, one of America's largest financial institutions, has lor
an MLB sponsor, minor league sponsor, and supporter o
League Baseball USA. Baseball is part of its DNA. In the s

of 2006, I assisted Bank of America as we mounted a campaign to raise money for the Little League Urban Initiative. It raised money through an internal summer campaign to refurbish fields, start new leagues, provide equipment, and more. I applaud Bank of America for its leadership.

But it's not just the Fortune 100 companies that should be involved with Baseball United. There are other large and mid-sized corporations in the United States that are seeking to transform their image, and a campaign transforming baseball's image would be a perfect connection. Every business can benefit from the sense of integrity that baseball (in its post-steroids era) brings to the table. Waste Management is a company that specializes in the hauling and recycling of trash. This same company is currently involved in the reclamation of green space in communities across the nation, so as to create parks and other ecologically safe and attractive areas to enhance cities and towns. Just as Dave Steiner, CEO of Waste Management, has done well to contribute to and also gain from such a positive movement, if the cause being led by baseball is real, timely, and substantive, companies looking for a corporate makeover with an exciting visible campaign would be wise to attach themselves to Baseball United.

And Baseball United is not just for corporations. In their song "Mrs. Robinson," Simon & Garfunkel sang, "Where have you gone, Joe DiMaggio?" Today, we could ask a similar question: "Where have you gone, Abe Stark?" Baseball has turned away from the mom-and-pop-sized businesses, of which Mr. Stark's clothing store is a classic example. Instead, the game has focused its attention on the Budweisers, Coca-Colas, and Chevrolets.

The result is that small business, which had been the mainstay of advertising in stadium signage and program advertising for decades, has been shunted to the sidelines. Only in minor league and youth baseball can you still find local businesses, small shops, and independent restaurants advertising in programs or placing their banners along the outfield walls. Baseball United could

provide an opportunity for small businesses to get back into the game of baseball at the major league level. Let me explain how that would work.

Today, it takes a five- to seven-figure advertising investment to affiliate with a major league team or advertise in its ballpark. That's why the advertisers you see in major league stadiums are national corporations or only the biggest regional businesses. But what about the little guy? What about the local small business that can't spend half a million dollars to plaster its name on the left-field wall? Such enterprises could afford an investment of perhaps $30,000 or $40,000. Right now, there's hardly a marketing avenue for a business like that to involve itself with Major League Baseball. This is a reflection of the fact that baseball as a whole has become increasingly sophisticated about attracting million-dollar and multimillion-dollar advertisers. But as a result of going after the big money, we've left behind all the businesses that would love the opportunity to connect with the game, and also would be crucial to the success of the game at the local level.

As we've seen, one of the key goals of Baseball United is creating more venues for young people to play the game. Kids need well-equipped and well-maintained diamonds in their neighborhoods, not to mention well-trained coaches and helpful clinics. It takes money to keep a baseball field in playable condition, especially if it gets a lot of use (and that's the whole idea). Local businesses are key players in providing the funds necessary to maintain local baseball. Their participation is just as important to the sport as Nike or Gatorade.

Baseball is a difficult game to conduct, but it also brings people together in ways that sports like basketball don't. A baseball game can be difficult to manage and pull together. Yet a great game of basketball just takes some blacktop, a basketball hoop, and a basketball, and you're all set. But with baseball, it takes a community. You can't just build fields and fail to maintain them—they'll turn brown and rot. It takes a full-on community effort to create and maintain baseball fields, to equip teams with balls, bats, gloves, uniforms, batting helmets, spikes, the whole package. Baseball offers the opportunity for partnership among kids, parents, community leaders, businesses, and government, in ways that other sports simply do not.

For example, I'm working with Randy McPhillips, an avid sports fan, a former Little Leaguer, and the owner of a mortgage company in Orange County, California, who wanted to find a way to give back. As a result, the Padres are collaborating with Mr. McPhillips to create a situation where we, in conjunction with the San Diego City Council, are revitalizing and maintaining a baseball field in an inner-city community that otherwise couldn't afford it. I would love to see Mr. McPhillips's example repeated across the country.

The Padres are partnering with business in a manner that benefits everyone—the business, its customers and prospects, neighborhood kids, and the game as a whole. Careful planning must go into such projects. Choosing the right recipient is as important as choosing the right donor. If you give people something for free, they tend not to place much value on it. The families that sign a commitment letter to agree to maintain and protect the use of the neighborhood field gain a sense of ownership for that field. Businesses that come into the MLB family as a sponsor or underwriter can receive game tickets for clients and also gain opportunities to get their names publicized and become a part of the baseball machine. Community contributions become investments with positive returns for all.

Instead of one such small-business sponsor, we as MLB franchises could bring in dozens of such businesses. This would deepen and solidify our ties in the local business community.

It certainly takes more effort to find multiple small-business sponsors at $10,000 to $40,000 each than it does to nail down one corporate relationship worth $2 million to the team. But the effect of these small-business dollars on baseball's relationship to young people and the community could be absolutely electrifying. Businesses would be thinking about baseball. Businesspeople would be taking their clients and their families to games. A new generation of players and fans would arise as a result of these refurbished fields of dreams. And the MLB team itself would have generated enormous waves of goodwill.

One such small-business deal can pay for the salary of the individual in the front office charged with creating and maintaining these small-business accounts, and that person can then go out and develop dozens more. Multiply this effort by the thirty MLB teams and suddenly you find an entry point for hundreds or even thousands of small businesses that previously could never have paid the freight to involve themselves at the luxury-box level of corporate sponsorship.

Give these businesspeople opportunities to meet and greet the players. Let them share in the glory when the local ball-fields, to which they have contributed, have their opening ceremonies. And don't be shy about creating media opportunities around these community-outreach events.

CHAPTER 8

The Fans

It's not an easy time to be a baseball fan. The game has suffered so many blows over the last twenty years, from labor strife to Pete Rose's gambling scandal to steroids and the ever-increasing cost of tickets, not to mention the appeal and lure of other sports and entertainment options. A day at the ballpark is still a lot more affordable than an NBA or NFL game—there's no doubt about that. But when you attend a game today, you definitely get the sense that a lot of hands are reaching into your pockets, whether they are selling you high-priced parking and concessions or a wide range of expensive souvenirs. But the charms of the ballpark remain eternal. You'll remember your first baseball game for the rest of your life. The challenge is to build on that experience and to support the game within your community.

Another factor that makes baseball an increasingly difficult game for fans to feel passionate about is free agency. As I've discussed, free agency doesn't give fans a chance to get to know the players very well, because players are with a team for only a few years, and then they're gone.

The NBA and the NFL do a much better job of marketing individual marquee players as representatives, not just of their team, but also of the league as a whole. Kobe, Shaq, Yao Ming, Brett Favre, Peyton Manning—these players stand not just for their individual teams but for their entire leagues. Their star status transcends an individual franchise even with high-profile troubles following many of them. As a result, fans feel a sense of kinship to the NBA and the NFL as sports entities in a way they don't with Major League Baseball. Jerseys with those players' names are hot properties.

There are dozens and dozens of star baseball players playing today. But how many can you name that represent more than their team franchise? How many of those you know would you want your son to emulate? Somehow the Yankees get the lion's share of publicity for baseball, partly because they play in the media capital of the nation, partly because their payroll is invariably the highest, and partly because, well, they're the Yankees, the all-time winningest organization in baseball. Even the casual baseball fan could probably name three or four Yankees off the top of his head. But what about players on other teams? How many members of the 2005 World Champion Chicago White Sox can you name? (If you live in Chicago, this question doesn't apply to you.) How many St. Louis Cardinals can you name? How many Atlanta Braves? Houston Astros? Detroit Tigers? And these are the better teams!

Baseball players—even many of the best ones—seem to be playing out much of their careers in relative anonymity, unlike forty or fifty years ago when baseball players had bigger international names than the president. Today, you could be standing in line at an airport or hotel lobby next to a quality Major League Baseball player, and you might not recognize him. If you were standing next to Kobe, LeBron, or Shaq, you'd certainly recognize the star at your side (the height would help, of course).

Instead of spending more time marketing individual players, Major League Baseball has tried to gain more fans and keep the ones they have by building more attractive ballparks. And you have to give MLB credit, because so many of the newer ballparks are really beautiful landmarks—AT&T Park in San Francisco,

Camden Yards in Baltimore, Minute Maid Park in Houston, and, of course, Petco Park in San Diego. These new ballparks are often much more than a place to watch a game—they are self-contained entertainment centers with as many shops, restaurants, and bars as a good-sized airport. They are clean, safe places to enjoy valuable time with your family.

Fans do want a nice, comfortable place where they can take their families. Some older stadiums had rather small seats (the American fanny has, after all, grown over the decades), inadequate restrooms (especially for women), obstructed views, and other such factors that some baseball purists may call "charm" but other people find unappealing. So it's great that we've got all these new ballparks, but unless fans are given the opportunity to develop a stronger awareness of who the players are—players who care and relate to their team and town—the baseball renaissance we're talking about will remain elusive, nothing more than a dream. People will attend because it is an available entertainment option, not because they love the game.

While a new ballpark may not be the panacea for Major League Baseball, it certainly can make a huge difference for a city. In San Diego, the building of Petco Park, a multiuse facility, has led to more than $2 billion of revitalization in the city's downtown. The ballpark is the hub and the catalyst of San Diego's redevelopment, and the proof is in the fact that you see cranes in the sky everywhere you look in the city—new offices, retail space, and residential homes. Yes, they built a new downtown mall, and yes, they built a convention center. But it wasn't until the ballpark was created that downtown San Diego really took off.

The same can be said of many of the other major league cities where ballparks have returned to their downtown roots—Baltimore, Cleveland, Milwaukee, Pittsburgh, and San Francisco come to mind. Even minor league teams are getting into the act. Today, a typical minor league ballpark can cost $20 to $30 million to build, and minor league team owners are recognizing that the best way to recoup an investment like that is to develop or redevelop as much of the land surrounding the ballpark as possible. From a business point of view, creating a new ballpark does a lot for the surrounding city. But the ballpark itself is not and cannot be the answer when it comes to reconnecting with fans. Only a greater emphasis on the player-fan connection can accomplish that.

Whenever there's a new ballpark, fans flock to it for the first couple of years, whether the team is good or bad, just because they want to see the place that everyone is talking about. But after time, unless management is fielding a competitive team, more and more fans come to the ballpark dressed as empty seats. A baseball stadium may be an architectural gem, but ultimately, people don't relate to buildings in the same way they relate to the players—especially those who can run, field, hit, throw, and win at the major league level. What happens to a building ten years down the line is hardly as interesting as what happens to a human being.

A recent Harris poll caught my eye. It showed that twenty years ago, baseball was considered the number one favorite sport by 23 percent of all sports fans in the United States, trailing football by only a percentage point, but leading pro basketball, golf, hockey, and all other sports. Today, only 13 percent of sports fans consider baseball their favorite sport—that means that almost half of those who favored baseball have shifted their allegiance to some other game. Now, it may just be that the pie of available sports/entertainment dollars has been increasing so much that there's plenty of room for NASCAR, golf, arena football, and all these other sports to exist without threatening baseball's bottom line. But at some point, you have to believe that if more than half of baseball's fans no longer consider it their favorite game, baseball has to be leaving a ton of money on the table, money that these other sports are rapidly and happily absorbing. Fans are concerned not only with the stadium but also with what's going on in the field. The haughty, pampered attitudes of the players do not go unnoticed.

Months ago, I was corrected when I mentioned to one of my fellow executives on the Padres that I was headed down to the locker room to have a talk with the ballplayers about an upcoming Negro Leagues event that we were hosting. The executive told me, "Dave, it's no longer called the locker room. It's the *clubhouse*."

There's a vast difference between having a locker room and having a clubhouse. When I think "locker room," I think about a bunch of guys who have come to work hard and play hard. A locker room evokes the sounds and smells of the locker rooms from your college or high school days. Maybe they weren't the most up-to-date, refined facilities. Maybe they smelled of liniment oil and Magic Shave—or worse. But when you were in the locker room, you were preparing to play—no matter what it smelled like.

Now, a clubhouse—that's a different deal. When I hear *clubhouse,* I think of a private golf club, or a luxurious spa. I see myself lounging in a thick terry-cloth bathrobe, padding around in slippers on plush carpet meant to absorb unwanted sound, indulging myself in an overall atmosphere of gentility and ease. The locker rooms of my day are gone, replaced by the *clubhouses* where players can unwind on leather sofas propped in front of forty-two-inch plasma televisions before and after a game.

Just the difference in terminology demonstrates the change between the way players used to be treated and today's players—who feel a sense of entitlement that comes with donning a major league uniform. With the high salaries comes celebrity treatment, making ballplayers more like movie stars. If anything, the players sometimes act just a little too comfortable for my taste. There's a lack of intensity and passion exhibited on the field when players don't hustle out to their positions at the top of an inning or don't run out every hit. I respect the need of a player to look cool—uniform style and all—I wouldn't want to take that away from anyone. On the field, I always wanted to look good, too. But there's a subtle distinction between looking cool and looking like you just don't care about what's going on. Sometimes I get the feeling that the money that flows with such abundance has made the players feel a little too comfortable and a little too entitled, turning off fans in the process.

I certainly hear this from friends of mine who are major league managers and coaches. The players are often making many times more in salary than the managers, and the managers say that today's players are much harder to motivate. There's that dreaded sense of entitlement, the sense of "where is mine?" and "I don't need to listen to anybody; sit me out if you want because I got paid already." It's great for the ballplayers' individual bottom lines, but listless baseball players don't really make for an entertaining spectacle, let alone a successful game or even a successful sport. This behavior makes it even harder for the fans to relate to and admire the players, and if they cannot relate to the players, they're not going to feel as connected to the institution of baseball.

Let's compare the typical major league game today with what I saw in March 2006 during the World Baseball Classic, which consisted of an array of international teams not jaded by the affluent world of MLB. There, players were hustling, laying down bunts with precision, giving themselves up for the good of the team, and looking as excited as a bunch of Little Leaguers who had somehow found themselves playing before a major league crowd. I don't mean to generalize about major league players, but I do have to question the intensity that many bring to their efforts on the field.

Remember, fellas, it's a privilege to play the game—not a right. So play it right! Fans can tell. Fans know the difference. Even casual fans who may not know the intricacies of the game can certainly discern whether players are acting like they're fully interested and committed to what they're doing. Mix in drug use, shameful headline-making behavior, and a you-can't-touch-me attitude, and we are headed down the wrong path. Fans really want to attach themselves to players who play with passion. When was the last time you were at a major league game and said, "I'm not going anywhere right now because I don't want to miss my favorite player at bat."

Pete Rose's nickname was "Charlie Hustle," and for all his faults, he gave fans full value for their entertainment dollar. It's not often you can attach the word *hustle* to players today.

But when the major league minimum salary in 2007 is $384,000, the average salary is approaching $3 million, and private jets are waiting for players before All-Star Games are even completed, it's sometimes hard to listen to somebody telling you how to improve. Giving the players less money wouldn't make the situation any better, and that's simply not going to happen. Honestly, I'm not sure that there is a solution to this problem. It's just the evolution of the sport. The answer has to come from within the heart, soul, and character of each player and from the leadership and culture of each ball club. If they are all serious about the game and their commitment to the fans, they'll go the extra mile.

Different eras in baseball history have different names. There was the dead-ball era of the 1960s when pitching was king, and lately we've been in the era of the assisted home run, thanks to a litany of the game's top players. My concern is that baseball has moved on to yet another era: the era of complacency. There's so much money in the game at every level that you have to wonder whether teams or players are completely invested in the idea of giving everything they've got to win—except in the playoffs, of course. Fans question whether both sides are giving their all.

Another issue confronting fans is the fact that the games have gotten longer as the American attention span has gotten shorter and the desire for immediate gratification has deepened. It used to be that the same pitcher would start and complete the game, or turn the ball over to one reliever in the eighth or ninth inning to finish. Today there are an endless number of pitching changes in the last three innings of a game, because of the specialization—perhaps the overspecialization—of roles. You've got the setup guy, the long-relief guy, the guy you bring in with two outs and two men on to pitch to a left-hander, and finally the closer. Each of those pitching changes consumes a lot of time because each constitutes a TV time-out.

Why are managers making all of those switches? They're doing so partly for strategic reasons—obviously they want to win, and they want to use all the tools at their disposal. But there's another dimension that managers won't tell you about. They need to appear to be thinking all the time! They need to appear to be strategic, so that the fan in the stands, the reporter in the press box, and the team's management can all say, "Look at our manager! He's pushing all the buttons! He's really thinking out there!"

Another reason games are slowing down is that there's simply more on the line because salaries are so huge. Every wrong move has a dollar sign attached to it. Everybody, therefore, is contemplating his next move a little more carefully—the pitcher on the mound, the batter in the batter's box, the fielders. The umpires are even judged on their strike zone by technology that is displayed on live television. They call a game judged by caution only, call pitches within the zone. The consequences are a smaller strike zone and longer games—when an umpire's job might be on the line. Baseball was always a strategic game, but now it has taken on even more of the attributes of chess—if I do this move, will they counter with that, and then if we do that, will they do this? Everybody's thinking seventeen moves down the chessboard, which might be great from a strategic point of view, but it can be deadly to the casual fan. The last time I checked, nobody was paying any money to watch players and managers think. They want to see action; but with all those breaks, the last three innings of a baseball game can take eons.

Another concern of fans today is the disparity of wealth among teams. Baseball has always been about the haves and have-nots, and somehow, through the decades, it always seemed as though the Yankees and a few other teams had more than anyone else. Today, there is revenue sharing, although the process is still so new, although we are seeing new champions consistently—perhaps the playing field is leveling out. Yet we can't be sure whether the smaller-market teams are reinvesting their revenue-sharing dollars in quality players or simply banking that money. When you look at some of the lower-payroll teams, it certainly raises the question as to where that revenue-sharing money is going. If fans suspect that owners are not doing everything they can to put the best possible team on the field, they won't support the team.

Why do people love the NBA playoffs, the Super Bowl, NCAA March Madness, the Masters, or the last few laps of a NASCAR race? Because they have the sense that the competitors are giving everything they have. Admittedly, the long NBA season can lead to halfhearted performances, but most NBA fans who attend games feel they get their money's worth. There's always some spectacular "above the rim" moment that makes you glad you were there. The same applies with the NFL, when some player gets hit so hard he's out of commission. Yet when you go to a Major League Baseball game and you see guys who are making eight or ten million dollars a year not running out every hit, it's only natural that you'll get disillusioned with the game. It's up to all of baseball's constituencies to create a situation where fans will want to come to the ballparks. With the right competitive atmosphere and a renewed fan interest in more personable, communicative, and giving ballplayers, baseball can surely become America's favorite sport again!

CHAPTER 9

The Parents

When was the last time you looked around and saw parents playing catch with their children?

This was a staple activity for families long ago—the first step toward enjoying the game of baseball—but today, that beautiful image is all but memory. First, many children are raised in one-parent families, and that one parent is either out working or simply too tired to have a game of catch. Second, our kids are glued to screens—TV screens, computer screens, Game Boy screens, you name it. They are not participating in sports nearly as much as they are developing the muscles in their thumbs, sampling every snack available, enjoying a sedentary lifestyle, and generating flab in the midsection. We are raising a generation of kids with the greatest hand-eye coordination in the history of mankind . . . as well as the highest rate of obesity and the worst level of physical fitness ever.

We've got to get parents to set a better example for their kids by taking better care of themselves and by "getting physical" with their kids—spending quality time with them, taking them out to the park and playing ball. In our society, so many people are too busy pushing buttons and eating fast food to do anything that smacks of family togetherness.

I can tell you for a fact that that's not how it works in my

family. I'm having a great time teaching my kids the joy of playing sports, as well as the importance of good nutrition and education. If it works for me, it can work for you. More parents
should be doing the same.

You may not remember your first basketball or football game,
but you will most certainly remember the first time your dad
took you to a baseball game. And if you were a little kid whose
dad took you to Yankee Stadium, I've got good news for you: If
you thought that former Yankees were actually buried out there
in Monument Park, you're not alone. Just about every kid thinks
that! (Just for the record, they aren't.)

In 2007, the Padres are planning their marketing and community relations efforts around heightening awareness of health
and fitness for young people through baseball. I started down this
road some thirty years ago in San Diego, then in other cities
(with board-of-trustees stints on the Hackensack Medical Center in New Jersey, and the Morehouse School of Medicine in
Atlanta, Georgia), through my foundation, Health and Education
Through Sports (For Kids and Community).

Parents need to know that baseball is an unparalleled teacher of
some of life's most important lessons, including teamwork, leadership, personal fitness, overcoming obstacles, tolerance, and
continuous learning, to name but a few. Why do you think our
society uses baseball terminology so frequently in describing situations: "Step up to the plate," "Touch all the bases," "You hit a
home run," and so on? The essence of the sport teaches us so
much about how we handle ourselves in a variety of life situations.

It's ironic that in the age of the Internet, when practically
every conceivable piece of information is at our fingertips, it's
harder than ever for parents to find accurate, useful information
about how to involve their kids in the game of baseball.

I'm proud to say that my hometown of St. Paul, Minnesota, has
been voted the best community in the nation for parks and recreation facilities, and San Diego is a close second. What are these

communities doing that could serve as models for the rest of the nation?

When I was growing up, it was a simpler time. Practically every kid played some improvised form of baseball on the open fields, front stoops, alleys. Almost every kid on my childhood team lived within walking distance of the ball field, and only a couple of the kids had to be driven by their parents or rode their bicycles. The result was that we all got to the field on time for practices and games, and if you were late, you were in trouble.

My experience wasn't uncommon. It was easy to find a game of baseball back then. All you had to do was go down to the local parks and recreation facility, and there were diamonds galore. Even where baseball fields were not accessible, a vacant lot or schoolyard or an alley would suffice, with a telephone pole acting as a base and a trash can acting as another. Kids used rubber balls, tennis balls, whiffle balls, broomsticks, or even broken and reglued wooden bats. They were creative and innovative with their free time, made up their own rules, and improved their game. It seemed as though everybody was playing baseball, not just in my home state, but across the country. They get more practice, fitness, and exposure to the game this way than through structured practices and games.

Baseball is and always has been a great game for kids. It's not as violent and potentially injury-causing as football. It doesn't leave you quite as exposed as basketball, where if there are shortcomings in your game, everyone is going to see them very quickly. It requires less endurance than soccer, which was barely on the radar of the America I knew as a young man. Baseball was simply a great game for kids to play. All the parents knew it, watched it, and could teach you something about it.

Today, by contrast, children and their parents lead much more structured, busy lives. As parents, we shuttle our kids from one enriching activity to the next. Family schedules have become as complex as space shuttle timetables. Many families now keep track of their members' whereabouts on electronic calendars like Yahoo! or Google. You can't even begin to count the number of after-school activities currently available. There are so many options for today's average kid that it makes a parent's head spin (not to mention the effect on a parent's wallet).

What's a parent to do? Naturally, I'd like to make the case for baseball, but it's up to parents to educate their children about the sport's many virtues. Let me provide you with the facts.

First, consider the case of a child who has serious athletic potential. Baseball is perhaps the toughest game to learn and takes a longer time to master. Even players who have been in the majors for years are still learning new things about their position and the way the game is played. Remarkably, as difficult as the game is to master, it may well offer the widest variety of young athletes the greatest possibility of a career in professional sports.

Precious few basketball players are going to make it into the NBA. It's tough to tell a kid that, especially if he is six one or six two, athletic, and has a decent jump shot. But we as parents should be able to face reality more easily than our kids. Even a six-foot-two athlete is on the small size for an NBA career, a league increasingly dominated by men six foot eight and taller. The number of spots for new NBA players each year is miniscule, especially in light of the millions of young people who aspire to pro basketball careers. Unless you are the second coming of Kobe Bryant or LeBron James, you may just have to forget it, or consider a career overseas. The NBA is indeed for the precious few, and the Europeans who bring a different style of ball to the United States are garnering many of those previously guaranteed spots for Americans.

A career in the NFL is also extremely hard to come by. Even by the time you reach the college ranks, you'd better be fast, you'd better be able to hit, and you'd better be able to absorb an enormous amount of punishment, because those are the expectations at the college level. In the NFL, the expectations are even higher.

Even with the few new positions that open up each year for players, competition is extraordinarily intense, with many careers often cut short by injury. Players are bigger, faster, stronger, and better equipped. The damage that football players do to each other is devastating—just take a look at the weekly highlights and injury reports on any given weekday during the NFL season. Football players on average experience far more serious health problems (joint damage, arthritis, and postconcussion effects) in their thirties and beyond than the rest of society, and they die younger. All this for a career that lasts on average just four short years. It's a tough way to go. That's why Hall of Fame coach Hank Stram called the NFL "Not for Long."

And then there's baseball. If your child is a four-tool or five-tool player—has the potential to evolve all of the key abilities of a Major League Baseball star—that's fantastic. But even if your child is a three-tool or four-tool player, he can make a fantastic living as a professional baseball player. Even if your young man has only two skills that could rise to the professional level—well, there are plenty of Major League Baseball players with much less ability who are pulling down seven-figure salaries.

One study suggested that the odds of a high school athlete making it to the NBA are approximately 800 to 1. The odds of a high school student making it to Major League Baseball are only 500 to 1. Still long odds, I grant you, but you don't have to go to Las Vegas to know that that's a slightly better bet.

How hard is it to beat those 500-to-1 odds? Tony Lucadello, arguably one of the greatest baseball scouts of all time, offers simple rules that allow every child to teach himself how to improve his game. These rules include properly positioning one's feet when fielding grounders, keeping your head up and your glove down, how to hold and throw the ball, taking one hundred grounders off the wall as fielding practice daily, and playing with enthusiasm.

It sounds simple, but it's not simplistic. Following these steps will help any young man stand out from his peers and get the jump on that coveted career in the major leagues.

I hear all the time from college coaches that the most athletic young men opt for basketball or football, with dreams of NFL or NBA careers fueling their passion for those sports. I'm not suggesting that nonathletic individuals are drawn to baseball. But the fact is you don't need quite the same level of athletic prowess to have a Major League Baseball career. I'm not saying that you can get away with incompetence; you do have to master certain baseball skills. The game is far too competitive for that. But we live in an era of specialization, where teams will pay dearly for individuals who can bring certain specific abilities to bear—the ability to get on base, throw, or play defense, to name a few.

Baseball is practically the only sport that accepts athletes with many different body types. Think about my old friend, the late Kirby Puckett. You might not have considered his appearance to be that of a major league player, but he could beat you in a dozen different ways, and he was rightfully a Hall of Famer. Joe Morgan is another Hall of Famer who came to the game height-challenged but twice emerged as league MVP. Both players were highly intelligent individuals with high baseball IQs. There are plenty of highly successful major league ballplayers who are not tall and rangy and who do not have the big, athletic bodies typically associated with professional athletes. Some guys don't even pretend to be in athletic shape. There are quite a few players who have managed to create an outstanding career for themselves even though by looking at them, you get the sense that they never met a doughnut they didn't like.

If anything, the trend in baseball is increasingly leaning toward nonfive-tool players, individuals who may not excel by the traditional measures of the game but whose specific abilities appeal to the *Moneyball*-era general managers. That book—*Moneyball: The Art of Winning an Unfair Game* (2003) by Michael M. Lewis—detailed the revolution going on in the front offices of Major

League Baseball pioneered by Oakland Athletics General Manager Billy Beane, which is the trend toward choosing players not based on their appearance or physical attributes but on their ability to contribute through some form of specialization such as on-base percentage (OBP). So much of this is happening because there are precious few multifaceted athletes participating.

So the level of physical competition is slightly lower when it comes to baseball. You can specialize in one area of the game and go on to have a lucrative major league career. Parents need to know these facts, because the possibility of having an MLB career may be within the grasp of many young men who would have no possibility of making it in the NFL or the NBA. There's nothing easy about baseball—don't get me wrong. Even an average fastball is thrown in the ninety-mile-an-hour range, and it travels the distance from the pitcher's fingertips to the catcher's glove in less than half a second. That's not a lot of time in which to react, and you're not exactly playing in the same pristine environment as a professional golfer at Augusta. You're playing in a noisy, jammed ballpark with tens of thousands of fans screaming at you. You're all alone facing the pitcher, just you against nine guys, and you've got to somehow make contact with that ball—the single hardest act in sports—hit it where they ain't, and then run like hell. That is no joke. You also have to deal with repeated failure: sixty-five to seventy-five percent of the time you're going to make an out instead of getting on base. Coping with that much failure in front of that many people isn't easy. But don't let me drive you to a sports psychologist. I'm just giving you the facts.

I'm not saying that it's *easy* to make it as a Major League Baseball player. All I'm saying is that in today's world, it's *easier* for a young man to embark on the road that may lead to a professional baseball career than any other sport. You'll probably last longer physically and make more money as well.

The problem is that today, *baseball is simply hard for kids to find.* Parents often have to drive many miles in order to find a place offering

Little League for their kids. There's a very good reason for this: Park and recreation departments perform cost-benefit analyses on the use of fields. They know that they can transform a large baseball diamond into two soccer fields on which more young people can play, or into countless basketball courts that don't require significant maintenance and require little organization or money to create leagues. Kids' soccer is so strong financially that it often funds park and recreation departments' transformation from baseball diamonds to soccer fields.

At the same time, the park directors see reduced demand for baseball, partially because popularity for all the other sports has risen so dramatically in recent years. The people running park and recreation departments can do the math. Smaller budget, fewer people interested in baseball, combined with more parents wanting their kids to play soccer, means that you see a lot more soccer nets and a lot fewer pitching mounds. And once you *do* find a team or a league, it's harder to work those games into the increasingly complex schedules of parents and students when you have to drive to everything. (I'm a parent, trust me—I know!)

Parents also encounter resistance from their kids when they suggest trying baseball. The kids often say that the game is boring, or they tell their parents that their buddies are playing other games, or they say that it's hard to learn. If parents are armed with correct information, they can work to overcome those arguments. Incidentally, the best time for kids to learn to love baseball is *before* they enter Little League, when play is free, unrestricted, and fun.

One factor that turns kids off to all organized sports is the manner in which an increasing number of parents behave along the foul lines. The pushy, loudmouth parent has become a cliché in our society. You see them everywhere—screaming at their kids, acting in an overbearing manner, shouting at the umpire or the coach. Often, parents hammer at the coaches and umpires, disputing calls, demanding that their son be hitting lead-off, pitching more innings. This upsets many kids, and rightfully so. Who wants to be around when your parent, or someone else's parent, is acting more like a child than an adult?

In Little League and other organizational leagues, there are now seminars to teach parents how to behave in the stands. One of the best independent seminars is run by my friend and colleague from the University of Minnesota, Frank White, whose seminars can be found at www.respectsports.com. White, the manager of recreation programs and athletics for the city of Richfield, Minnesota, has devoted his entire career to teaching and promoting the benefits of coaching and refereeing in sports and recreation. Today, he offers tips for parents on how to foster a better playing environment, and how communities can remain in control of their youth sports programs. He breaks down exactly what are healthy expectations for kids of various age groups. "Keep things in proper perspective," he tells parents on his website. "It's only a game!"

It may only be a game, but tell that to the legions of Little League parents in our society who treat every game between their fifth-graders as if it were the seventh game of the World Series. Abusive parenting has become such a problem in Little League that the organization now devotes an entire web page to the problem, and even offers a "Parents' Code of Conduct" as part of its Parent Orientation Program (www.littleleague.org).

The Little League websites tell parents: "While many parents are often very enthusiastic when watching their child's games, it is important that you do not get overly involved, taking personal offense to official calls or decisions made by coaches and umpires. Most of the time, these decisions are made in reference to official game rules that you may not be familiar with." They also ask parents to take a pledge that includes the sentence "I will positively support all managers, coaches, and players." Isn't it astonishing that we have to teach *parents* the concepts of fair play and decency before we can even reach the kids?

We shouldn't have to live in a world where parents need seminars to be taught not to use foul language toward other parents, children, or the umpires and coaches, who are either volunteering their time as a community service or offering their skills and knowledge for minimal or no pay. The best thing a parent can do for a child who seeks the enjoyment and personal growth of youth sports is to not only help the child learn, adapt, improve, and enjoy his or her participation, but also for the parent to learn how not to discourage a child from wanting to play in the first place.

Another concern I have today about the way young people play baseball and other sports is the limited amount of practice they get in addition to the limited amount of free time they spend with creative or offshoot baseball games. They need to play, run, throw, chase, and catch in informal, unstructured, and unsupervised practice sessions. You do this often enough and you begin to understand the nuances and develop the reflexes for the game and you are able to overcome obstacles. Parents, if you can find a place to show your kids some of these games—and kids, if you learn to play them on your own—they will go far.

When I was playing, we would usually have a number of practices in between games. Today, kids show up for games without having done the slightest bit of practicing, and the results show on the field. Baseball is a game of skill, reflexes, instinct, and experience, and these attributes are gained not during games but primarily during practice sessions and free playtime. Of course, today nobody has any time for anything as mundane as practicing baseball. It would require another round of scheduling for all the parents, and the parents barely have time to deliver their kids to the games, let alone practices. At the same time, these parents and kids want to experience the accolades of the games. But they've forgotten about the blood, sweat, and tears of practice that it takes to improve and grow. I see too many kids who can't play, have no instincts or reflexes, and yet want to be a hero on the field. It won't happen without knowing the rules and practicing diligently.

In my day, kids simply took thousands or even tens of thousands more swings than kids do today. The bats were wooden, a lot heavier, so we developed better strength, quickness, and coordination than kids with today's aluminum bats. We practiced all aspects of the game—fielding, bunting, sliding, stealing bases, rundowns, tag-ups, you name it—and many of these skills have practically become lost arts. You can practice any of these skills in improvised play with as few as three friends using any kind of bat or ball and a couple of gloves.

You see the results of this lack of practice at the major league level where some of the younger players can't lay down a bunt, hit the cutoff man, hit behind the runner, or perform any of the other myriad tasks that were drilled into baseball players of previous generations during countless practices. It comes from watching their role models in MLB, and from shortcomings in youth coaching. Hot prospects today often come with very little minor league seasoning.

The same player who might have spent a couple of years at the AA level and one season at Triple A before getting his call up to the big leagues today might find himself facing major league pitching after being promoted directly from the lower minors.

It's all very exciting for the young player, but if his skills were not honed in practices dating all the way back to youth baseball, that player has little chance of sticking around for anything longer than the proverbial "cup of coffee" in the majors. For every successful young major leaguer, such as a Frankie Rodriguez today or an Al Kaline forty years ago, there are dozens more young players who come up to the majors too soon and simply do not have the skills to last, and their careers are over before they know it. We are not doing our kids a service by failing to provide them with the practice time they need in order to make it professionally, or to develop good habits for other walks of life. They need more practice time including unsupervised play to advance their skills. Without this play, a young player may never develop a love for the game. His paid incentive alone does not allow him to develop a love for the sport. My rule of thumb is that the young player should be practicing at least four to five times as much as he plays. That's how difficult the game is to learn. If your child doesn't engage in this play, you should understand that he is behind in development.

As challenging as baseball can be to master, it offers so much. It is truly a team sport and the friendships you make are deep and long-lasting. Parents, wherever you are situated, you are the ones who have the greatest responsibility to inform your children about the possibilities baseball represents. You are their greatest coaches. If they don't hear about their options in baseball, they may well not learn about them anywhere else. As baseball has diminished in popularity, more players have gravitated to the rival sports of basketball, football, and soccer. You even hear that kids gravitate to extreme sports because they do not like coaching and are attracted to the creative, individual element of those sports. When they retire from their playing days, they become coaches in those sports. This is especially true in the inner city, where there are fewer coaches to be found. So become educated . . . and educate your children. You can make the difference for them, guide them toward physically fit and healthful lifestyles, and perhaps give a little push toward a college scholarship or a legitimate shot at a professional career.

CHAPTER 10

Community Outreach

On all but one of the official websites of the Major League Baseball teams is a link for "Community." If you click on "Community," you'll find some examples of how that team is serving the community in which it is located. You might find a golf tournament featuring former players that benefits a particular charity, or a canned-goods drive sponsored by the wives of the players, or information about visits the players make to area schools and hospitals.

It's all good. I would never criticize the charitable efforts of others, nor would I impugn anyone's motives. However, I have several concerns.

Today, Major League Baseball has a basic website template (MLB.com) that each team uses, with slight variations. On those websites, you'll find scores, standings, the team's schedule, ticket information, and that aforementioned link, "Community." That word appears on each MLB team website in the same place. Each team essentially "does its own thing." While the basic theme of community outreach holds true from team to team (whether it is under the aegis of marketing, their foundation, or community relations or outreach), the manner in which teams express their desire to serve their communities varies.

Contrast the homegrown feel of the Community section with

the uniform way teams market themselves through the schedule and ticket-buying options on the MLB sites. It is up to the club owners to decide which charitable endeavors they want to pursue locally. There's nothing haphazard or optional when it comes to creating revenue. In fact, 98 percent of the teams' websites are homogeneous, marching in lockstep one with the other, leading fans in exactly the same way through the ticket- and merchandise-purchasing process. As a result, the financial success of MLB.com is indeed flourishing.

There's nothing wrong with quality sales marketing. One of the most important themes of this book is that baseball isn't doing nearly enough to market itself properly. But what does it say about the importance of community activities if you visit a team's website a hundred times and never even notice the Community link? And what does it mean that the Community section of the teams' websites is the only section that is not rigorously controlled by Major League Baseball? It means there's no top-down campaign.

Baseball as a whole sees community outreach primarily as an afterthought, something not worthy of the standardization inherent in every other facet of the teams' websites. I'm not saying that teams don't care. They do. Each team does wonderful work in terms of connecting with its community. But many initiatives require more muscle. MLB is the leader—individual organizations can lead if they choose to. The extent and impact of the clubs' efforts are also limited when there is not a hundred-percent consensus buy-in and participation by the athletes and the players. But if certain efforts were standardized under the directives and outlines of a campaign such as Baseball United, the game could carry its commitment to communities a lot further.

Not only is community outreach fragmented, with the exception of a few dedicated teams, but few efforts have anything to do with the game itself. Most of the outreach could be performed by any community-minded group. For example, golf tournaments are fun and give fans a chance to mingle with retired players. However, it would be more beneficial to use an activity that would make people feel more connected to baseball. I'm not talking about throwing out the other existing activities or employing crass, underhanded means of using community-service activities to sell tickets, but let's take advantage of community-service opportunities and creatively use them to reconnect our communities to baseball, and help the game endure.

It's not enough for baseball to support community and charitable organizations, as important as those ties are. Baseball has to be in the business of preaching baseball every chance it gets—and this means that a greater portion of community outreach efforts should combine doing good works in the community with reigniting the passion for baseball. Major League Baseball can do better with its public relations and positioning, as other sports do. But again, few people listen. It doesn't matter what you do if the public is not hearing the united voice of players, owners, and MLB.

In addition, baseball practically buries its good deeds by bundling them all behind a tiny, unglamorous, one-word link on its page, without offering the slightest explanation of what might be found there or why it would be worthwhile to visit that page.

By contrast, take a look at the NBA's main website (www.NBA.com). In the lower right-hand corner, you'll find a large box dedicated to the "NBA Cares" program. The NBA is extremely conscious of its image, perhaps because it has faced so many challenges to the squeaky-clean image it seeks to project. In a recent two-day period in 2006, the NBA Cares portion of the site showed a large picture of NBA star Kevin Garnett about to enter a game, with a young boy crouching beside him. Behind Garnett and the young man is a banner that stretches practically the length of the court, honoring the NBA's commitment to Hurricane Katrina victims. The caption read:

The Timberwolves' Kevin Garnett sits with a young evacuee displaced by Hurricane Katrina as he waits to enter the game during Kenny Smith's Hurricane Katrina Relief NBA Charity Game September 11, 2005. Garnett was recently named the 2006 recipient of the J. Walter Kennedy Citizenship Award, presented annually by the Professional Basketball Writers Association. The award is named for the second commissioner of the league and honors an NBA player or coach for outstanding service and dedication to the community. As part of his Hurricane relief efforts, Garnett donated $1.2 million to Oprah's Angel Network to build 24 homes, one house per month for the next two years.

The next day, the NBA Cares box showed a picture of Michael Redd at a healthy-eating program in a Christian school. The caption read:

Michael Redd of the Milwaukee Bucks high-fives students following his presentation at the Healthy Kids Wellness Is Now! program at St. John's Lutheran School in Glendale, Wis. The program, designed to provide youth in grades 4–7 with information on healthy eating, exercise and healthy life choices, gave students the opportunity to write a 250-word essay describing their healthy activities.

Below the captions were three links, the first to an auction of various basketball-related items to benefit the National Center for Missing and Exploited Children. The next link was entitled "Basketball Without Borders," referring to the global basketball development and community-outreach program, which, according to its web page, www.nba.com/bwb, returns to four continents this year and will be staged in Lithuania and Puerto Rico for the first time.

Basketball Without Borders has featured one hundred twenty NBA players, coaches, and team personnel from twenty-nine teams as camp coaches for seven hundred young athletes from nearly one hundred different countries and territories. "The NBA family and campers have traveled more than eighty-five million miles and logged more than one million hours of community service" since 2001. You can read about the good works that Basketball Without Borders does on its website in English, Lithuanian, and Spanish. With a program like that, who needs the United Nations?

The third and final link in the NBA Cares section ties the NBA to Penguin Classics, the website of the publisher of classic novels. Here, you find basketball players and their favorite books. Ray Allen, for example, recommends *Siddhartha*. Allen says on the website that "*Siddhartha* is a book about discovery, and it affects every person a little differently. But everyone who reads it is affected. That's a classic." You learn about Allen's basketball career and his Ray of Hope Foundation in Connecticut, which provides food and clothing for the needy. Next comes Becky Hammon, the WNBA star, who recommends Arthur Miller's *The Crucible*. Hammon says of Miller's work, "When you read a book like *The Crucible,* you get a whole new perspective: in this case about persecution and politics, and you can think about it in terms of what you see in the world today."

I quote these websites at such length not because the NBA is a perfect role model for all major sports; indeed, the NBA, like all major sports leagues, has its share of fights, fracases, and image problems. Some have said the industry almost gets a "free pass" even with the havoc some of the athletes have created. But whose jerseys are they wearing? If NBA stars were lemmings, a whole lot of people would be going over the cliff. Instead, I share this information because I want to demonstrate just how thoughtful the NBA is with regard to its community outreach, which has expanded past the borders of the United States and spread onto other continents. Not coincidentally, its marketing machine has been spreading its wings across the globe. But the most important fact to realize is that the NBA is committed to its programs and is not afraid to let you know that it cares, sharing with its fans, in an easy-to-find location on the main page of its website, the varied good works—both basketball-related and not—that its associates perform each and every day.

Baseball can learn a lot from the NBA Cares program, the name of which is plastered on all the players' seats and is highly visible throughout the playoffs, which are broadcast around the planet. Baseball must learn that it also has to coordinate its community-outreach efforts in an across-the-board manner. But baseball cannot just be serving the community. It has to be making the community aware of the greatness of the game and its players, just as the NBA does with its efforts. Baseball should take a leaf from the NBA's book and promote the efforts of teams and individual players in a much more effective and visible way. This is not a time for baseball to be modest.

What I admire so much about NBA Cares is that they have tied their community work to the specific issues that most relate to their core audience of young fans. In just the two days alone that I've referenced, they targeted disaster relief, children's nutrition, and literacy. Would the NBA truly care so much if it did not have to contend with the perception of an image problem, due to the trouble that some of its ballplayers create for themselves? Hard to say. But no matter what the motivation, the end result is that they have brilliantly tied their community outreach to the issues that most affect the next generation of NBA fans—and they are not shy about telling the world of their good works.

Baseball has to recognize and capitalize on its greatest asset: its players and their ability to connect the generations—an asset that separates the sports. Today, football, basketball, and even NASCAR and extreme sports dominate the landscape. But the reality is that each of these sports is a relatively new phenomenon as a focus of national attention. It wasn't all that long ago that the New York Knicks, in order to entice fans to come to games, had to give away a free Harlem Globetrotters ticket along with a Knicks ticket. It wasn't all that long ago that Super Bowls didn't sell out. "March Madness," the term that describes the NCAA basketball tournament, was simply not that big a deal until the mid-seventies. And NASCAR? Don't even ask. I could go on to mention that the NHL had only six teams instead of thirty as recently as 1967, but you get the point.

Down through the years, there's been only one sport that has truly captured the imagination of generations of fans, and that's Major League Baseball. You could argue that boxing was often as popular or even more popular than baseball, depending on who the champion was and the quality of the contenders he faced. Yet boxing has waxed and waned in the imagination of the American people and has truly fallen by the wayside in both the number of fans and respect for the sport, while baseball has remained the one true sporting passion in our nation, until it began to get shouldered to the sidelines by the variety of other sports that everyone follows today.

Baseball has the history and the statistics, which carry both weight and reverence. It's the oldest of American sports, and organized baseball stretches back to the 1870s, making it fifty years older than football and approximately ninety years older than the NBA or any of its predecessors. Historically, baseball icons have been bigger and more universally noticed than those of other, more recent sports. As for auto racing, the first car would not be driven in America until baseball had been played for more than a generation. Baseball also enjoys a statistical continuity that no other sport can match. The NFL's Competition Committee meets yearly, to change the rules to favor offense or defense, as marketing needs dictate. Seemingly every year, the NBA brings in new innovations to make the game safer, more exciting, more offense oriented—or all three.

The advent of the twenty-four-second clock in 1954, and the three-point shot in 1979, has made it impossible to provide meaningful comparisons of statistics from one era of the game to the next. This is where baseball shines. As Barry Bonds's pursuit of Babe Ruth and Hank Aaron attests, it is often possible to make meaningful statistical comparisons of baseball players who lived and died decades or generations apart from one another. It's as hard to stroke three thousand hits now as it was in Lou Gehrig's day, and it's just as hard to hit .400 or hit safely in fifty-six consecutive games as it was in the era of Rogers Hornsby and Joe DiMaggio. Even as the game changes—designated hitters, specialization among relief pitchers, advances in equipment and training—the essence of baseball remains the same.

This is the heart of the matter. This is the asset upon which baseball should and must capitalize in order to regain one of its roles in society: its ability to provide continuity among the generations. Baseball's community outreach ought to focus on this theme of "connecting generations" in every possible way. We all have cherished memories of going to a baseball game with our parents or grandparents. We all remember what it was like the first time we saw the inside of a major league stadium—the endless swath of green grass in the outfield, the brick, mortar, and iron of these vast sports temples, the hard-hitting and hard-throwing athletes (and you'd pick a favorite or two to follow), the first home run we ever witnessed in real life. These memories constitute uncapitalized assets on baseball's spiritual balance sheet, and on baseball card collections that would imprint the name, face, and statistics of your favorite forever. For baseball to play to its strengths, it needs to convert those untapped assets into something tangible.

To that end, baseball also needs to continue making efforts to honor its past—distant and recent. Fans love the retired players from the era of their childhoods—not just the great players whose names are legendary, but even those players who might have contributed one important home run, a single well-pitched game, or a long throw from the outfield during a championship season. People in their late thirties, forties, fifties, and older tend to relate more to former players than current players. They grew up watching players of my vintage, owned those players' baseball cards, and may be more on the same page culturally with baseball players on their side of the "generation gap."

In New York, they bring back players for what are called old-timers' games, but I think the term *Legends Games* is a little more enticing. Few want to see old-timers, but everybody wants to see legends. Teams around the country should make greater use of their alumni, many of whom may still live in the area. There should be one or more Legends Games in every Major League Baseball stadium every season, because that would be a way to attract the older generation and corporate leaders, and keep a continuity of fans returning to the ballparks.

But we mustn't stop there. I also propose monthly Generations Days at the parks, where multigenerational families of fans are honored for their continuous devotion to the game. On Generations Days, we'd post photographers at every entrance to the stadium, snapping pictures of grandparents, parents, and children as they make their way into the park dressed in jerseys from different eras—and have these photos flashed on the JumboTrons and Diamond Vision screens during the game. Retired players living in the area—whether they played for that particular team or not—would make great ambassadors on Generations Days, creating excitement and joy for the fans by going from section to section or greeting those who rooted for them so many years ago. Likewise, team stores should be stocked with their artifacts and memorabilia, signed and unsigned.

I leave to others the idea of how to strategically conceptualize Generations Days for their respective communities, whether to offer discounts on tickets, and what other celebrations might occur, but I think the basic idea is sound. Baseball connects generations, and we should trumpet that fact at every ballpark many times during the season.

Baseball can also connect with the various ethnic communities by planning events that hit home for these distinct groups of people. It can, for example, bond with the African American community by tying in games to family reunions. The African American community is especially receptive to the idea of large, multigenerational family reunions, which can span a long weekend and involve dozens or even several hundred relatives at a single spot. Baseball could propose special family reunion packages, offering nearby park space as a venue as well as attractive group discounts. Family reunions bridge the generations; so does baseball. It's a natural fit.

Finally, baseball needs to spend more time honoring its history. It is said that ten thousand members of the Greatest Generation—those who served in World War II—pass away each and every day. I know this because the San Diego Padres, residing in a military town, have their own military marketing department—perhaps the best in MLB. Other clubs can learn how to recognize and serve this group from the Padres' experience. Baseball's greatest generation—the individuals who broke the color line as they followed in Jackie Robinson's footsteps—are of the same age as our World War II fighters, and many of them did in fact participate in World War II, Korea, and other conflicts. Baseball needs to be much more cognizant of the pioneering roles these gentlemen played. They not only displayed enormous courage in integrating the game, but they made the game better as well—more athletic, more acrobatic, more competitive, and more fun for the fans to watch.

Just recently in San Diego, we put on our third Negro Leagues Recognition Day luncheon, which honored some of the great players now in their seventies, eighties, and nineties. We had young women dressed in 1930s-style clothing escorting each of the former players into the luncheon to standing ovations. We heard speakers who talked of those long-ago days and how they paved the way for players like myself to find a place in professional sports. On the field, we were able to provide Buck O'Neil and the Negro Leagues Baseball Museum with a check for $39,000, which we raised, through the sale of artwork, as a charitable donation toward the Negro Leagues Baseball Museum, in Kansas City, Missouri (see www.NLBM.com). My friend Buck passed away as I completed work on this book, and I regret, as do all who love the game of baseball, that he was not given a place in the Hall of Fame in Cooperstown during his long lifetime.

MLB should establish and maintain a database of all living Negro Leagues players and should set a minimum standard at every major league ballpark for the annual recognition of those men while they are alive and can enjoy it. It should offer this information to each major league team, so that more of these gentlemen can be honored in their lifetimes, and so that they can share their experiences with current players and fans.

Most youth baseball community organizers are not aware of the fact that former Major League Baseball players are available as speakers. If you visit the Major League Baseball Players Alumni Association website, www.MLBPA.com, you'll find that among the marketing and charitable endeavors they are involved in, there is also a list of former players who will add luster, excitement, and big league experience to your next Little League, PONY League, or Babe Ruth League event. The players are out there, and they love to give these kinds of speeches. Sometimes a fee is involved, and sometimes not. But there's nothing like a major leaguer or former major leaguer to help sell tickets, bring in donations of all kinds, and make the day truly memorable, especially for the kids.

Don't let anybody tell you that today's baseball players don't care about their communities. They do. There are countless major leaguers who make significant contributions of time, money, and in-kind services—some publicly, some privately. They have followed my lead, either by establishing foundations to help their communities or by establishing "knothole gang" arrangements that provide hundreds or even thousands of young fans with bleacher tickets.

After extensive research, soul-searching, and strategic thinking, I came upon a very public, nationwide issue that our industry has a chance to champion. I refer to the challenging health issues of childhood and adult obesity and the chronic illnesses incurred by Americans with sedentary lifestyles. Since obesity is recognized as the biggest health and economic problem facing America in the twenty-first century, this is an easy campaign for baseball to run with. Our kids are less fit than ever, and they need direction from the role models they respect and the sport they love to change their behavior.

In 2006, an article in *USA Today* noted that 20 percent of America's youth are obese, 17 percent are newly obese, and kids are developing chronic illnesses that only used to appear in older people. A report on NBC suggested that this is the first generation of kids that will die at an earlier age than their parents—all due to physical inactivity and poor nutritional habits. My suggestion to Major League Baseball, the Players Association, and the players: Grab this very important issue by the horns. Work together for the cause, not just for a short while but on a long-term basis. Change the lives of children and their families, and watch the growth of respect, admiration, support, and corporate sponsorships, for the game.

The problem is that Major League Baseball isn't getting the word out about our community accomplishments. Yes, MLB's favorite charity is the Boys and Girls Club, and the Players Association Trust's focus is on volunteerism—both notable and worthwhile causes—but these don't resonate with the nation. I hope we are wise and quick enough to adopt this concept. Again, it won't happen until baseball is truly united in the task. They must put aside their egos, and give credit to the people who do good. I would love to see Major League Baseball borrow from the "best practices" of the NBA and other major sports leagues, or better yet, follow the prescription that I've discussed. If America is going to care about baseball the way it used to, then baseball needs to get the word out that it cares about America and that it honors its own past even as it celebrates its own success. Connect the communities to the game, connect generations of fans through the game, and baseball will make great strides toward a truly historic comeback. The risk is low and the reward is high.

CHAPTER 11

The Government: Federal, State, and Local

Baseball, its leaders and players, took a serious hit in public relations in 2005, when it was admonished, threatened, and had the curtain pulled back by Congress in front of the nation. Ideally, that shouldn't be the role of the federal government. The federal government should be considering other, more pressing issues, such as the national budget and security, instead of addressing drugs and sporting issues. But there are no hard feelings between Major League Baseball and the government. There shouldn't be. Although they prefer not having to work too closely together on any issue, they can use each other's strengths to visibly and wholly dedicate themselves to positive causes such as youth initiatives that keep kids active, safe, healthy, and involved in their communities. Congress has prompted change in the relationship between players and the MLB; and it has played a primary role in helping baseball clean itself up. The two groups should continue to link arms in an effort to help not only baseball but American society to grow.

On the state and local level, governments have to refuse to be held hostage by owners threatening to move unless they receive more money, percentages, a new ballpark, or other financial perks—usually hundreds of millions of dollars of tax breaks or, worse, taxpayer dollars—whenever a stadium lease is about to end. The owners are making money, with increased revenue from baseball marketing, revenue sharing, or through capital gains upon the sale of the franchise.

I urge owners and local politicians to take the lead in getting budget money to support baseball efforts in their states and areas, and for creating public/private partnerships that help further sports (particularly baseball) in their home states and other areas as well. Baseball signifies activity, fitness, saving parklands and green spaces, keeping kids out of trouble, and bringing families closer together and making communities stronger.

I would also ask our representatives to help establish laws that would make it unlawful for sex offenders and child predators to work for parks and recreation departments, coach youth teams, or for them to come within a certain distance of these facilities, just as the law stipulates for schools. Children need safe places to play, and parents want to have a little more faith that their neighborhoods and youth sports programs are monitored and safe.

State officials can call for legislation, or use of funds (in partnerships) for communities to refurbish and reestablish baseball facilities like we've done in San Diego. If you are an elected official, know that baseball's flame has not gone out. Be in touch with the youth and collegiate organizations, such as the Little League, Urban Initiative Program, or the College Baseball Foundation (www.collegebaseballfoundation.org), or the professional team in your area. Search the list of community programs that can be partnered with to help baseball grow. MLB will pay attention and find a way to make it happen through one of its existing or contemplated programs, such as its work with the Boys and Girls Clubs of America or its own Baseball Tomorrow Fund.

The last time Major League Baseball crossed paths with the federal government, the event took place under the harsh glare of television lights in a congressional conference room. The topic was steroids. Major League Baseball players, looking uncomfortable in their business suits and ties, came under sharp questioning from senators, who seemed to be just as anxious to appear to be "doing something" about the steroid problem in baseball as they were to be posing next to the baseball stars they were giving such a hard time.

Ironically, the whole thing worked. In the time since that hearing, in March 2005, few well-known Major League Baseball ballplayers have been busted for steroids. Once-huge bodies are returning to normal size, balls are not flying out of parks at unprecedented rates, and there are very few players of note today who are under suspicion of taking performance-enhancing drugs. Those who did use them have no doubt quit. Indeed, baseball scouts sometimes note in their reports that various players have been "caught by the government," a jocular reference not to an arrest but simply to the fact that the threat of government intervention caused players to lose the steroid-induced extra bulk.

The steroid problem will most likely never completely go away because there will always be some players looking for any edge to boost their careers. My primary purpose in this chapter is not to discuss steroids, human growth hormones, and other performance-enhancing drugs, but to discuss what constructive role government at all levels can play in Baseball United. I would love to see the government-baseball relationship move beyond the media circus and the adversarial stance that characterizes the connection today. Instead, there is so much that government can do if it were to play a part in Baseball United. I'm never comfortable discussing subjects that are out of the range of my experience. That's why you're not going to find a treatise here on constitutional law, the antitrust exemption, or other topics that I will leave to those better placed to address them.

When I first began to think about what the federal government could do in order to enhance the game of baseball, I began to wonder whether the federal government had any business at all in promoting a sport. I don't think we send elected officials to Washington to think about the vitality of certain sports. But the fact is that the government does stick its tentacles into just about every aspect of modern life, and that even includes sports and fitness. Sports and fitness, after all, positively affect our youth, improve the nation's health, and build strong communities.

The President's Council on Physical Fitness and Sports has designated May as National Fitness Month (www.fitness.gov). If the government is going to be involved in promoting fitness, then it should do so in a way that actually affects people and creates a high level of awareness. If you're going to do it at all, do it right. And when I have the ear of the president again for a moment (and he is a baseball man!), I will suggest that the President's Council reorient itself toward baseball. Baseball games, drills, and practices require involved, active youths.

As I've discussed, the values that baseball teaches are precisely the values that young people—and adults—need to develop in order to lead successful lives: teamwork, healthy lifestyles, communication, patience, practice, the development of skills, and, above all, hard work and the ability to deal with setbacks without quitting. Not everything in life goes the way we want, and our capacity to endure disappointment and defeat is just as important, if not more so, than our capacity to handle success. There's no better game than baseball to teach great values to our kids.

The physical skills that baseball players hone are ones that practically every individual possesses (although admittedly not on a major league level). Just about everyone can run, throw, catch, or make contact with a baseball. Compare this to football, where not everyone can throw a perfect spiral, let alone be of the size and strength to tackle another player. Baseball offers the best mix of values and athletic skills, and wouldn't it make sense to have baseball as the preferred vehicle for teaching these mental and physical attributes to the nation? Most important, with our nation swiftly moving deep into obesity due to the lack of physical activity, baseball, nutrition, and exercise could play an important role in combating this national crisis.

I'm not suggesting that other sports don't have enough to offer to become the centerpieces of a national program. But does everyone in the country really want to play football? People love watching the proverbial "car wreck." Hit or be hit: Is that a value that we want to teach young people? It's certainly not a tactic that will attract the nation's young female population. In contrast, softball is one of most popular sports for girls.

There's more aerobic benefit in going outside and playing catch than people realize. You don't have to be able to throw a strike from deep center to home plate to reap the benefits from playing catch. And yet how many of us do so? That's yet another simple, enjoyable skill that translates into the athletic range of the average American, and it's at the heart of baseball.

Stretching is an oft-overlooked aspect of any physical conditioning program. It's not enough to run regularly; you've got to keep your body limber through a sensibly organized stretching program. Every successful athlete knows this, but you have to wonder how many "weekend warriors" develop injuries, either on the basketball court or the running track, simply because they didn't take the time to stretch properly. Now think for a moment about spring training. The quintessential photograph that you see in the newspaper is of guys in their uniforms, lying on the grass on a ball field in Florida or Arizona, stretching their torsos, while the rest of the nation is still shoveling snow. Baseball players know a lot about the importance of stretching. Put it all together and you can see why a focus on baseball, and baseball-related athletic skills, would be a natural fit for a government organization seeking to encourage people to take better care of themselves. Under Baseball United, I would invite the federal government to reengineer their efforts, including revamping the President's Council on Physical Fitness and Sports toward a baseball-oriented curriculum. I'd also move National Fitness

Month—and I admit the first *I* ever heard of it was while I was doing research for this book—from May to April, to coincide with the beginning of baseball season. That's a time when most of us need to think seriously about our physical fitness. The ground has thawed. We've hopefully recovered from the physical abuse of the indulgences of Thanksgiving, Christmas, and New Year's, and we've also come back to reality from whatever impossible New Year's resolutions we may have set for ourselves.

From the perspective of Major League Baseball, this would be a great way to build interest in the game and create goodwill. Excitement for the game is at its highest. Unlike at the end of the year and postseason, all thirty teams are in the pennant race. Fans and media everywhere are energized. Making baseball and its players the leaders in a national movement toward better health is a logical step in helping adults set a better example for kids.

The number one problem in our nation's health system is childhood and adult obesity—the basis for chronic and debilitating illnesses. Kids are not nearly as active as they used to be, they do not eat right, and they do not understand nutrition and health issues. Portion control is out of hand in the home and in restaurants. We are only now seeing trans fats eliminated from public restaurants and food products on the shelves. Children are developing adult forms of diabetes at an alarming rate, and some health experts predict that the poor diet and lack of exercise that afflicts much of our nation, the affluent as well as the indigent, will result in an epidemic of people in their twenties suffering heart attacks and strokes. Perhaps baseball, in partnership with the federal government, can lead the way to positive changes in the health of the nation.

In 1987, in *Turn It Around: There's No Room Here for Drugs,* I wrote about the importance of creating healthy alternatives to the troubled lives that so many of our adolescents and teens lead.

Since the time I wrote that book, these societal ills have only worsened. That is why I partnered with Hackensack Medical Center in New Jersey to develop the Dave Winfield Nutrition Center to help people make healthy lifestyle changes. There's nothing like getting people out, moving their bodies, playing games, and experiencing the joy and pride of physical fitness. You have to give them an alternative to sitting around in front of the TV, playing video games, and eating snacks, or, much worse, getting into drugs or other serious kinds of trouble.

Lemon Grove, California, Little League recently celebrated its fiftieth anniversary with a dedication ceremony and field renovation including the installation of a new playing surface with grass infield and outfield, the installation of a sophisticated irrigation system, new fencing, and an electronic scoreboard. Those amenities didn't just happen by themselves! They arrived as a result of a collaboration among Little League International's Urban Initiative, the Padres, the San Diego County Board of Supervisors, and lots and lots of community volunteers.

Here's where government and businesses can work together. I would like to see states and localities offering tax breaks to businesses that reclaim parcels of land and turn them into green spaces, parks, and baseball diamonds. Does your company sell sporting goods? Lighting equipment? Sod? Cement? Tractors or mowers? Are you in construction? There are so many different aspects of developing and maintaining baseball fields. Surely your organization can help out. Or, if you are a professional, your legal, accounting, or insurance services would be most welcome. We live in litigious times, and everything and everyone has to be protected. Many organizations have volunteers, including AARP, and anyone can be a resource and volunteer as a coach and offer support. I'm not just asking you to open your heart and your checkbook. I'm asking you to take action. The return on investment that you and your company will receive is immeasurable. State and local government can help. Will baseball take root everywhere? I doubt it. You've got to have the right soil, the right seeds, and the right climate conditions. In this case, start at the bottom and grow it—through example—to the top. Can government till that soil? Can they put their money and influence where their mouth is? Absolutely.

CHAPTER 12

Colleges and Universities

College baseball programs have just about everything you could think of that's necessary for turning out potential Major League Baseball players. They've got the equipment, the coaching, the facilities, the enthusiasm, the competition and lengthy travel schedules, the academic foundation, and all the other ingredients required to bring young athletes to a level of maturity, experience, and ability that takes them that much closer to the pro game.

NCAA schools have about eighty sports programs for men and women, and all of them have varying limits on scholarships they can give. Basketball and football are the sports that make real money for colleges and universities. Even at top programs like USC and Texas, baseball is actually a money-losing proposition. With the advent of Title IX and the evolution of women's collegiate sports, there's been even less money for sports such as baseball, that do not contribute to an athletic department's bottom line.

Lack of money is actually a serious problem for many schools. Most can offer only a limited number of half scholarships (a maximum of 11.7), but more than that, schools below the level of the Southern and Southwestern powerhouse teams—such as Florida State, Clemson, Arizona, Oklahoma—find themselves in decline. They don't have enough money to keep up their facilities, and thus they become less attractive to top players. The fewer top players they attract, the more player performance declines, which means there's less money for facilities, which means the program becomes less attractive, and so on. It's a vicious cycle.

How bad is the money problem for many schools? Well, the University of Southern California has an annual baseball budget of $1.5 million. The team brings in $750,000 in revenue, so someone—the school, alumni, friends of the team—makes up that three-quarters-of-a-million-dollar shortfall *every year.* As a result, they have been a perennial powerhouse. For historically black colleges, by comparison, the baseball budget is so small that the travel and recruitment budget is often as low as three thousand dollars. USC might spend that much money on one recruiting trip! Historically black colleges, such as Southern University or Florida A&M University, simply cannot find and recruit enough African American players, and even the most famous black universities are fielding baseball teams that are no longer predominantly African American, but a mix of black, white, and Latino.

I've addressed the limited number of African American players, but the unfortunate phenomenon has particular bearing on college and university baseball programs. It's easier for a ballplayer to get discovered, signed, and nurtured in a tiny hamlet in the Dominican Republic or Venezuela than in an inner-city neighborhood or a black college in the United States. The rules are so different. In the United States, an MLB team is not allowed to sign a player until he is eighteen years old, or has completed high school. With the existence of college baseball programs, there's less reason for a team to sign a player at eighteen. At that age, he's still four or five years away from the major leagues. Developing a player in the minor league is expensive. It's more cost-effective to let him go to college, even for a few years, to develop mentally and physically, and then sign him in the draft when he's nineteen or twenty. This involves less of a gamble. By contrast, in the Dominican Republic, you can sign a ballplayer as young as sixteen; that's not including the many fourteen- and fifteen-year-olds the buscones sign under the table. The reality is that major league clubs often have players tied up at fourteen. And developing these players in their native country is not as expensive.

But college programs can't be depended on to develop the innumerable kids in this country—African American and otherwise—with pro baseball potential. Financial and scholarship limitations simply make it impossible.

If the program is going to provide a scholarship to a player, it has to feel fairly certain that this young man will be able to handle college life—the social aspect as well as the academic—and not just his role on the baseball team. Baseball coaches are looking for much more than physical maturity from the young men they recruit. They ask other questions as well: Does he have a good attitude? Does he get along well with other people? Is he coachable? Will he be able to handle the academic load? Will he stay out of trouble? Will he get along well with his fellow players and his coaches? Will he be able to handle the physical and emotional stress of a travel schedule that consists of a sixty-game season? Will he make it through the four years?

You've got to wonder whether college head coaches, who are almost entirely Caucasian, have the same comfort level with African American students that they do with white kids. If you asked any coach, he would tell you, "Race isn't a factor. We look for the best player available, and if that kid has five tools, I don't care what color he's painted. We want that kid." But there are few travel teams, baseball factories, or strong leagues in the inner cities, and coaches and MLB scouts are hesitant to hunt for talent in those concrete jungles. I would also suggest to all college coaches who run camps and clinics over the summer, to please make some local and regional contact with the coaches and leagues to get recommendations for quality African American players with college potential. Provide a camp scholarship or two for these guys and you just might find a diamond in the rough. That one opportunity might be all they need, and you've opened to diversity, which can only make your program better.

I'm not suggesting that we've in any way returned to the overtly racist past. Instead, I'm suggesting that a subtler process may be at work here. You can't legislate a comfort level, and you can't legislate subconscious feelings. Maybe there's nothing more to the dearth of African American college baseball players than the issues we've already discussed. But maybe there's something more, and that's the disturbing possibility.

You really do have to ask how it could be that out of the top sixty-three college baseball programs in the United States, not one has a head coach of color. Statistically, that figure just makes no sense. I could understand if you told me that there were only two or three out of those top sixty-three teams. But zero? It's 2007. Is it possible that there are no African American assistant coaches being groomed for head coach positions? Is it possible that there are no African American, former pro players who wouldn't be extremely excited to coach at the top collegiate level?

I'm not suggesting a conspiracy on anyone's part. Rather, it seems more to be a question of unconscious attitudes. Collegiate baseball can be considered the ultimate "old-boy network" in sports. The baseball fraternity is alive and well, and if you are a player or a former player, you're inside it; if you aren't, then you might as well live on the moon. This extremely tight-knit fraternity does a very good job of "looking after its own," and when a job is to be filled, there is always a large enough talent pool from which to draw simply by considering your old teammates and opposing players.

I've got to wonder why the network that creates a talent pool for baseball jobs would not bring about a situation where even a single African American would find his way into the head coaching position at a top program. It's not much better in football, according to a recent NCAA report. Outside the Historically

Black Colleges and Universities (HBCU), only 16, or 2.6 percent, of the 616 NCAA football teams have African American head coaches, even though approximately one third of the players are African American.

It seems fairly obvious to suggest that the NCAA become cognizant of this issue and take action to remedy it. I'm not talking about forcing schools to hire particular people. Instead, I'm suggesting that colleges and universities should be required to interview a certain number of ethnically diverse candidates any time there is a head coaching vacancy, the same rule that is practiced when hiring head coaches in the NFL. Unfortunately, the NCAA has chosen not to do this.

Yes, I'm sure that the practice in the professional ranks has led to the occasional sham interview, in which a candidate of color with zero chance of getting hired is brought in. And I'm certain that the same sort of thing would happen if the NCAA were to mandate a specific number of interviews with African American coaching candidates. At the same time, such a rule would broaden the pool of candidates to include individuals who might not be in the old-boy networks or might not otherwise come to the attention of athletic directors or other individuals involved in the hiring process.

It's entirely possible that if there were more African American coaches, you might end up with more African American players. But not because the coach would be "taking care of his own" or giving scholarships or roster spots to undeserving minority candidates. Every coach wants to win, and the best way to keep your job is to keep winning. So it's highly unlikely that kids of color who do not deserve scholarships would suddenly find themselves on teams where they don't belong.

Instead, it all comes down to comfort level. An African American coach may well have a higher comfort level with an African American player than a Caucasian coach, and vice versa. It seems hard to believe that we could still be having this kind of conversation about race six decades after Jackie Robin-son and four decades after the Reverend Martin Luther King Jr. but if the light needs to be shined on this topic, then let it.

The next issue to tackle is how to bring promising players of color to the attention of college teams that do not have travel budgets. Thanks to the many years of work of the Major League Scouting Bureau, and now the existence of the Internet, if a young player is playing baseball and is good enough, no matter where he lives in the country, people will know about him. They'll know that he is capable and well thought of in his region. But if that young man is in Florida and your school is located in Wisconsin, would you be willing to offer a scholarship based on a few lines you read about him on the Internet? Probably not, especially if you have the same limited number of scholarship dollars as most colleges and universities.

The business world has sought to step into this breach, and there are a large number of companies that offer websites pur-porting to connect young players with college coaches—in all sports. You can find these sites pretty easily by searching online for terms like *college sports recruiting*. For a fee, of course, these sites will post video and text about a player, telling the world who he is, what he has accomplished, and what his aspirations are. In theory, college coaches use these websites as tools for developing lists of players to recruit. But like anything else in the business world, there's the good, the bad, and the ugly. Many of these sites may not be able to deliver on all of the promises they make, in the same way that dating services on the Internet may overpromise and underperform.

I'd like to propose something entirely new: a not-for-profit company that specializes in providing video and biographical information on African American players at the high school level. Perhaps it can happen through the MLB Urban Youth Academies. The site would not require a significant financial investment from the players, who would be videotaped demonstrating their baseball skills—hitting, hitting for power, running, throwing, speaking in an interview, and so on. Sufficient video, as well as verification of academic ability, of each player would be posted to allow intelligent recruiting decisions to be made. In addition to the video, scouts could find information about each young man's baseball history: the teams and leagues in which he has participated, whether he has been on any traveling teams in showcase games, and other vital information.

This would have to be a not-for-profit venture if you want pure, unadulterated information on players. However, it could also be developed by someone as a for-profit enterprise; that is not out of the question. But I'm not proposing a way to make money, just a way to get information about ballplayers to colleges and universities that the schools would consider entirely aboveboard and accurate. We're not looking for situations where a player gets special placement simply because his family has paid more money. Instead, we're looking for democracy of placement based on a meritocracy of talent. We want baseball coaches in every corner of the country to have access to meaningful information about players whom they might not otherwise choose to recruit, along with contact information so that they can ask questions of coaches about the intangibles.

In order to establish a not-for-profit website like this, there are two ways to go. One is for major league players to contribute, just as Torii Hunter has gathered other major leaguers of all colors to provide financial support to deserving projects. The MLB Academy, whose first location was in Compton, California, is a great place to start.

The other option is to invite the NCAA itself to create, fund, and maintain this vital project. This is a systemic problem—and a systemic problem requires a systemic response, which is why the NCAA exists. It would be great if the NCAA were to study this problem and create the kind of website and talent posting system I'm suggesting. With the imprimatur of the NCAA behind it, college coaches would find the material on the site trustworthy and thus would have greater confidence in spending precious recruiting and scholarship dollars on players of color they might not otherwise have a chance to meet.

I recently attended an intraconference game between two collegiate baseball rivals, and the attendance was forty-eight hundred, a very large number for a college baseball game. By contrast, college football games at the major powerhouses—the Alabamas, the Notre Dames, the Michigans—routinely draw eighty thousand fans and upward. It may well be that when Michigan plays Notre Dame, you've got forty-eight hundred people working the game! Baseball can't compete. Expanding the pie—carving out more dollars for baseball—is most likely not going to happen. Instead, colleges and universities have to find ways to work within their means to attract more players—and coaches—from more diverse backgrounds.

It used to be that a strong prejudice existed in Major League Baseball against players with college backgrounds. The hardcore, gruff-and-tough players and managers with farming backgrounds tended to view with suspicion those elite educated young men who came to baseball from the college ranks. That prejudice no longer exists. Baseball people know that colleges and universities can be great incubators of major league talent. The level of coaching is so high that kids come out of college with large amounts of skill, knowledge of the subtleties of the game, and maturity. Extensive travel schedules broaden players and make them far more worldly than their counterparts who remain "down on the farm." The attention of Major League Baseball scouts in the U.S. has shifted to the college ranks today and there is no turning back.

When I was still in my teens, I left Minnesota for two summers in the early 1970s to play with the Alaska Goldpanners, a collegiate league traveling team that started in the forty-ninth state and routinely traveled down the West Coast and into the Midwest, venturing as far east as Wichita, Kansas, and even to a tournament in Haarlem, Holland. Now, that broadened me! We ended up playing in international tournaments in Europe against teams from places I had never even heard of, such as the Netherlands Antilles and Nicaragua. I started off that summer asking, "Where is that?" I quickly found out for myself while traveling with the team. Other summer collegiate leagues include the Cape Cod League and the Basin League. More leagues can be found by referencing www.NCAA.org and HBCUconnect.com.

Mark McGwire, Randy Johnson, Jason Giambi, Tom Seaver, Tony Gwynn, and Luis Gonzalez also played in the Alaska Baseball League, often in front of crowds of no more than three hundred fans. They say baseball has its challenges—but how about finding a bull moose standing on your front doorstep after a game, or trying to catch some shuteye when the sun never sets all summer? I think I'd rather be approached by a bunch of kids with a dozen baseballs each to sign than one of those big creatures!

For rich experiences like that, college programs are the best places for young players to turn to. College baseball rounds out major league prospects. When they graduate they are no more than two or three years away from playing in the majors. By contrast, unproven high school players typically need four to five years in the minors before they are ready for the rigors of major league ball. So, remedying the absence of African American ballplayers at the collegiate level is essential if the MLB is to retain African Americans in any serious numbers. Eliminating this subtle yet highly pervasive second color line isn't just the right thing to do. It's a smart thing to do. It is necessary for the future of baseball. Good teams, programs, organizations, and businesses know how important diversity can be.

CHAPTER 13

Youth Coaches

I want to begin this chapter about youth coaches with a tip of the hat to all of the parents, community members, and other lovers of baseball (and all youth sports) who give so generously of their time to help guide our kids. Thank you. Coaches shape kids both on and off the field, more so than teachers, and they are figures most people remember for the rest of their lives.

To be a coach or an umpire in youth sports requires an enormous sacrifice of time and money, and often the only reward for one's efforts is the vitriol, verbal abuse, and even physical abuse on the part of parents who ought to know better. In an era of unrestrained parental emotion along the sidelines, dual-job families, and the high cost of gasoline, anyone who still manages to find the considerable time it takes to coach youth sports is truly a hero.

The fact is that our youth coaches, umpires, and referees are leaving the game in droves. Why would anyone want to stick with it, given the stresses they endure, the demands on their time, and the general thanklessness on the part of so many of the parents, who are living out their own dreams of athletic glory through their kids?

As a member of the Hall of Fame and as a winner of the World Series, I've had the privilege of being a hero to millions of fans. It's a great feeling, and if you're a coach, umpire, or administrator in any sport, you can be a hero, too—by winning, yes, but also by running a consistent program where kids learn, have fun, and learn life lessons.

The quality of coaching in our secondary schools is often not what it could or should be. Baseball is no longer everywhere, so there are naturally fewer good coaches, facilities, and programs. So, how do you train the coaches? I propose a Baseball United Coaches Project. Major League Baseball should be on top of creating training videos to show coaches how to teach all aspects of the game. So many coaches have jumped ship for basketball and football, particularly in the inner cities. The new and newly trained coaches have to be shown what tools they need, what resources they can call upon for equipment, field maintenance, fund-raising ideas, and, above all, what they need to do to make baseball fun and enjoyable for youngsters of all ages. If kids are not taught properly at an age when they can grasp the game and its skills and have time to improve in successive levels of playing, they'll quit. They'll say the game's too hard, or no fun, and go elsewhere.

A good coach has to know the game of baseball inside and out, and must have the ability to convey the elements of the game to players, all the while making reinforcement and repetition fun for the kids. Practices have to be enjoyable to keep kids engaged. Most coaches don't realize that the most important thing to do during a practice is to keep all the kids active and moving on the field, going from station to station, practicing drills of short duration, with little downtime. Otherwise, kids get distracted, moody, and bored. It's essential to keep the kids interested and excited about what they're doing. A kid who becomes bored after a twenty-minute break is going to be lost to the game. A good coach will condense practices and make them upbeat. He can even give kids awards in practice for various challenges, such as accuracy on throws or running the bases. If coaches can incorporate challenges and rewards into practices, the kids are going to have a much better time.

One seemingly forgotten but very fundamental part of coaching is teaching the kids to talk or "chatter" on the field. This communication is essential to playing a game with nine people on a field spread out over so many acres. How do they knit, mess, and move as one?

A good coach also knows how to organize a practice into a variety of stations so that each kid gets to practice all of the essential skills that go into making a complete baseball player—running, hitting, sliding, throwing, catching flies, bunting, and so on. They know to recommend use of a wall for practice and drills, sandlot ball, and other unstructured games for kids to play in their free time. Unfortunately, many kids aren't getting the training, encouragement, or knowledge they need to succeed in baseball. I hate to point a finger at the very people who are getting low or no pay to do an all but thankless job, but we just aren't giving the coaches the adequate training they need to do their jobs well.

It would be great if Major League Baseball—the commissioner's office, the owners, the Players Association, the teams, and the players—all got behind Baseball United Coaches Project and devoted huge amounts of resources to making it work. But ultimately, the people who will decide whether baseball deserves to regain its primacy are not those in the press box or down on the field. Instead, the real jury consists of the kids of America, because they are going to vote with their time and interest for whatever extracurricular activity they most enjoy.

We have thirty major league teams and hundreds of minor league teams. Under Baseball United, each of their ballparks can become venues for coach training, places where the coaches themselves will deepen their connection to the pro game and learn more about how to pass on their love of the game. I see this as a top-down initiative. Those at the top of the food chain should know best.

Major League Baseball now has a huge stake in USA Baseball (www.USAbaseball.com) with all its leagues, including Little

League, PONY, Babe Ruth, and American Legion. With its survival on the line, MLB has the responsibility to take charge of the process of training the trainers of our kids. A great example to follow is that of the Minnesota Twins organization and its outstanding Play Ball! Minnesota initiative. This program brings to the Twins' stadium hundreds upon hundreds of coaches each year and provides them with the latest methods and information, and a high level of training. They learn how to organize practices, how to bring out the best in different personality types, how to manage a game, and, yes, how to handle those difficult parents shouting at little Johnny down the first-base line. There are meetings, breakout sessions, tutorials, and exposure to the latest ideas about coaching the game. Coaches learn about the wide variety of training equipment that now exists, have the opportunity to discuss with each other what has and hasn't worked for them, and can find a sense of camaraderie with others in their field. Then, of course, they are guests at the game at the ballpark that night. With more excellent programs like this one, we'll be moving in the right direction.

Major League Baseball should devote significant dollars and time each year to replicating Play Ball! Minnesota, under the aegis of the Baseball United Coaches Project, in every major and minor league ballpark in the country.

I don't want to threaten the livelihoods of those who now crisscross the country, holding clinics and teaching coaching to coaches. There's a place for you in this endeavor. With the Baseball United Coaches Project, and with Major League Baseball behind you, it will be even easier for you to reach your goals of maximizing the number of coaches, and therefore kids, upon whom you have a positive effect. We're not talking about pushing to the side of the road all those who have devoted years to the fine art of training coaches for the game of baseball. We want to work with you to bring your message to a greater number of coaches, so that all may benefit from your hard work. My message to kids is the heart of the next chapter.

CHAPTER 14

Kids

I'd like to address three groups of kids: those who don't have a lot of athletic ability but like the game of baseball, those who do have some athletic prowess and want to get better at the game, and those who are considering going for a college scholarship or a career as a professional athlete. Whichever group you consider yourself a part of, baseball can add so much to your life. I'd like to share with you some thoughts about how to maximize your enjoyment of the game.

Once upon a time, it was practically a crime for a young fan to come to a professional game and miss batting and infield practice. This is something I touched on earlier; in days gone by, the teams opened the doors of the stadiums so that the kids could rush in, sit in the box seats before the "rich folk" arrived, watch their favorites warm up, and maybe get an autograph or even a ball. Those days are seemingly long past. Today, when the gates open, the players have often finished batting practice, and infield practice is extremely rare, so the kids seldom see or talk to a player. We're cheating our kids—and ourselves. A brief by-chance encounter and verbal exchange with a player would last a lifetime for a youngster. Now, kids don't think taking infield practice is important to their game. Pregame practice is a way of drawing fans and players closer together. It's part of the leisurely feel of the game that shouldn't get lost in our warp-speed world.

Years ago, it was also extremely common for everyone in the park—grown-ups and kids alike—to keep track of the game on scorecards, or score books that they brought from home or scorecards they bought that day at the stadium. Today, it's rare to find a young person who has the ability to score a game. Scorecards and stubs of past games were once treasured memorabilia. Today, what passes for memorabilia has a highly impersonal feeling about it. It's a signed photo, ball, or jersey that comes with a certificate of authenticity—but it just doesn't feel as authentic as stepping up to the player and asking for an autograph yourself. Today, many kids see sports memorabilia not as something to collect and treasure but as something to sell on eBay. I've even been told, "It's better than a job."

If kids are going to appreciate the game of baseball, they should have the opportunity to see their favorite players close up preparing to play. There are so many lessons to be learned in that setting. They need to know how to score games and read and understand box scores, so that they can keep track of what's going on and truly appreciate the nuances of every pitch, every move, and every switch the manager makes.

We need to recognize the ways in which our children's lives have changed, too. It used to be that young people could head out to a ball field and play games from dawn until dusk. That's no longer the case, as I've discussed. Parents have to protect their children from predators, especially in our inner cities, so they can't leave kids alone for hours, unsupervised and unprotected. Child services or the police would have a conversation with you if you did. No more sandlot baseball.

As a result, kids aren't even learning the basics. It's amazing to me that a large percentage of kids don't even know to grip a ball across its seams to throw it. They have terrible throwing techniques because they rarely play catch. Take the typical ground ball.

An astute player knows either to step forward toward a ground ball and play it on a short hop, or step back and play it on a long hop. The medium hop will eat you up. That understanding comes from the experience of having fielded thousands of ground balls over the course of one's lifetime.

But do kids in Little League know this? For the most part, they don't. They don't have enough practice time to learn these skills. So, you see, kids get into game situations where they might make zero errors in one game and ten errors in the next. They're not learning or growing because they aren't trained in the skills they need to develop.

It's not just about fielding ground balls, of course. There's also making contact with the ball, knowing when and how to tag up on a fly, knowing how to lay down the right bunt at the right time, knowing how to move to your left or right to field a ball, and so on. Many kids don't know what a balk is (and if you go to a ball game, you'll find that neither do many of their parents). They don't know how to lead off, get a secondary lead, or steal, because that is prohibited in many major youth programs. If you're twelve years old and don't know how to steal a base, you are way behind in your development. There is a universe of baseball lore and rules that young people today simply don't have an opportunity to learn. As a result, their growth in the game is stunted.

In a way, this is good news for a kid who is not overly athletic, because it means that the level of competition for the typical Little League game is probably not as intense as in travel ball or a basketball or football game. That's why I want to urge every young person, no matter his or her level of athletic prowess or fitness, to give baseball a try.

As many of us know, even the best major league hitters fail to get a base hit 70 percent of the time. We also know that one of the most difficult things that a person has to learn in becoming a mature adult is the ability to handle frustration and disappointment. Baseball certainly gives you both of those—in large doses—

all the time. It's a humbling game, which is part of its greatness. Kids, if Michael Jordan could barely hit minor league pitching, with all of his athletic abilities, don't worry if you strike out more often than you get on base. You just have to hang in there and find ways to improve.

For young people with the desire and physical ability, who want to pursue baseball either at the collegiate or professional levels, I want to point out the options you should consider and what you need to know.

An individual who seeks a baseball scholarship may end up only getting a partial scholarship to college, but given the cost of education today, getting any kind of help can make a meaningful difference. So, if you like baseball and you're contemplating going forward with the sport, what do you have to do to succeed?

We live in an era of intense preparation and specialization. This is true whether we're talking about a kid taking a prep course for the SATs or a college student employing a service to help write his application for grad school. We've lost a lot of spontaneity in our society, and this trend is also felt in youth sports. It used to be that if a kid was athletic, he'd play football in the fall, basketball in the winter, and baseball in the summer.

That's what I did. I played baseball and basketball in college and was fortunate enough to be drafted by MLB, NBA, ABA, and the NFL. Would I have had the same opportunity today? Probably not. From youth sports through college, fewer coaches allow kids to explore their talents in multiple sports. They want commitment almost year-round to just one sport.

Unfortunately, this is the trend in all youth, high school, and collegiate sports. Competition is so intense today for places on varsity squads, both at the high school and college level, that coaches have a higher expectation in terms of a player's abilities and knowledge of the game. It's simply not possible to be an all-around player, competent at every sport, while mastering one in particular.

Kids are being forced to choose, often far too early in their athletic careers, what single sport they're going to play. This specialization often occurs as early as age twelve. At that age, you just don't know what sport you're going to like the most. Your body hasn't filled out, so you don't know where your strength will lie.

Specialization also leads to increased injury, as kids are practicing the same repetitive motions over and over without the variety of athletic movement that multiple sports offer. This is especially true for young pitchers, who are blowing out their arms in their early teens as never before.

The other downside of early specialization is that you don't learn the lessons that each sport offers. I didn't particularly love football, but I learned a lot about mental and physical toughness, which served me well in baseball. I did truly enjoy the game of basketball, and there's no doubt that running the floor in basketball gave me the aerobic capacity to roam the outfield, and the leaping ability developed by playing high school and college hoops helped me rob a lot of people of home runs.

Would I have been as good a baseball player if I had not enjoyed the exposure to the other sports and the experience I gained by playing them? Maybe not. So kids today face a cruel dilemma: They must specialize before they really know what they want, or where their bodies will be best suited, and then they don't get the benefit of playing—and enjoying—all the different sports available. They may become a baseball, football, tennis, or hockey player, but never a complete, well-rounded athlete. At the top levels, that matters.

There's not much I can do about stemming the tide of early specialization, but I write these words simply to make parents aware of the trade-offs involved. If your child doesn't specialize early on, he'll be competing against kids who did, for better or for worse. So what are you to do if your child is athletic and wants to pursue a career in baseball?

There are special programs across the country for kids who want to go further in baseball. Here are four.

The first is travel ball. There are approximately thirty-five thousand all-star/select/travel teams in the United States today, and they can be found across the country, but especially in warmer climates like the South, where you can play, if not year-round, then close to it. These programs are essentially intense baseball training camps, complete with practices, games, and pay-to-play tournaments. Some parents accompany their sons on these traveling experiences, while other parents entrust their kids to the individuals who run these teams. As with any program, it behooves parents to do their homework before sending their kids off with adults they don't know.

Some kids will travel with one or more teams over the course of a summer, playing as many as eighty to ninety games! That's a lot of baseball for a youngster, and that's where the seasoning comes if a player really wishes to advance. Colleges and pro teams regularly scout these traveling teams, and if you're good, news about you will travel. These programs do come with a cost, however. Parents have to pay for the privilege of having their kids play this much baseball, and not every parent can afford it. There is a cost to the health of a youngster as well—constant stress on developing limbs and joints and psyche can be traumatic and sometimes detrimental, causing debilitating injuries before growth plates are set. So beware, and make sure your child sees a sports medicine professional on a routine basis.

This is yet another reason why inner-city youth are at a severe disadvantage. Not only do they lack the facilities and equipment that are found in America's suburbs, but their parents often lack both knowledge of these programs and the wherewithal to pay for them. There's nothing easy about being an inner-city kid if you want to get ahead in the game of baseball.

The second opportunity for young players are the showcase games. These showcase games are located throughout the country, from North Carolina, Florida, and Texas to California, and are heavily scouted by colleges and the pros. Some games are invitation-only, while others are pay-to-play. If you're serious about your baseball future, you've got to find showcase games where you can hone and show off your skills to an audience filled with individuals who could make a considerable difference in your baseball future.

There's another phenomenon in the world of youth sports that did not exist when I was playing: sports performance institutes. These organizations teach kids skills of the game and also provide body-specific physical training to maximize the likelihood of success at the college level and beyond. One such program advertises on its website that it offers kids training in these areas: speed, agility, and coordination; strength and power; mobility and flexibility; and injury prevention. Kids as young as twelve are signing up to attend these institutes. If you've got aspirations to play at the college or professional level, this is the kind of commitment you have to be prepared to make.

When I was playing, the attitude was "Hey, let's play for enjoyment and fun. Maybe one day I'll get drafted." It's a different world now. Today, you can find information on the Internet about the pitch velocity of any given fourteen-year-old in Alabama. The *average* salary of a major league ballplayer is $2.7 *million*. The top guys make between $18 and 25 million. Back then, you had to be a superstar to make $100,000 a year. Parents can do the math. An increasing number of parents are willing to make that "up-front investment" in their kids' athletic future, because the rewards, from a partial college scholarship all the way to a major league salary, are so great. Parents today don't just let their kids go to public school without tutors and hope that one day they'll be admitted to Princeton. They do everything they can to give their kids an edge. That's what's happening in baseball, too.

Historically, every college baseball program has had a summer camp or clinic for aspiring youths. Parents might do well by having their youngster enroll in one or more of these programs. It's good to have your name, face, and skills come to the attention of a school you may want to attend. College coaches are using this method more and more to look for recruits. They cannot afford to travel the country on recruiting trips, so this works well for them.

While we're talking about all these new and often expensive approaches to training, let's not overlook the basics. Kids can also take advantage of such teaching tools as training videos, hitting off a tee into a net, or practicing soft-toss hitting, learning to keep their eye on the ball, developing the quickness and eye-hand coordination that's needed. It doesn't matter how much your parents spend if you're not willing to put the time in and take those tens of thousands of swings necessary to develop into a real hitter.

The unique thing about baseball is that it's not about trying to outrun somebody bigger and faster than you. Baseball allows you to showcase your own strengths, whether they involve hitting, getting on a base, stealing bases, fielding, throwing, or pitching. Aggressiveness, baseball instincts, and high IQ can help you shine as well. Kids, while you're waiting for your parents to write the big checks to put you in those showcase games, you can demonstrate to them—and to yourself—your own level of interest. Throw a baseball off a wall and teach yourself glove-work and footwork. Don't just wait to line up at practice and have your coach hit balls to you. Basketball players dribble and shoot baskets all day long to get better. You can do the same with a wall, ball, and glove. You develop arm strength and accuracy by throwing a ball off a wall, and at the same time, you develop foot speed and soft hands to improve fielding prowess. You'll start seeing immediate differences.

The more you practice, even by yourself, the more developed your baseball instincts will be. In George F. Will's outstanding baseball book *Men at Work: The Craft of Baseball,* Cal Ripken Jr.

talks about how he would begin to move in the infield even before a ball was hit, depending on what part of the plate the pitch appeared to be heading toward and who was in the batter's box. People who don't play the game don't understand how Ripken was able to make many of the tremendous plays he made. "How'd he catch up to that ball?" fans asked. "It looked like he was moving before it was hit!"

He *was* moving, because he *knew* where it would be hit. This involves watching catchers' signals, knowing the setup and the count, the batters' tendencies through the scouting reports, and so forth—skills built over time. If you're serious about the game of baseball, these are the sorts of skills and understandings of the game that you want to be learning.

Another piece of advice I offer young players is to key in on one particular baseball player, perhaps someone who reflects your own size or your own speed, maybe someone who plays for your favorite team. Zero in on his career. See how he handles everything from success to slumps. This can be an extremely enlightening process, and it will be very exciting when you finally get to meet that player (which will be a lot easier, thanks to Baseball United!) and talk about the game and life experiences with him.

Do you know how to keep the score of a game on a scorecard? If you're serious about your future in baseball, you should. Understanding baseball statistics is vital if you're going to make a career of the game. Averages, on-base percentages, slugging percentages, and the like are critical bits of information for any coach or team. This is what baseball's top brass increasingly do, and what they look for in talent. Visit ballparks—as many as you can, big and little, old and new. There are some grand old ballparks and some beautiful new ones to see. Learn the history. Learn to respect the game by visiting museums like the National Baseball Hall of Fame in Cooperstown, New York; the Negro League Baseball Museum in Kansas City, Missouri; or the Babe Ruth Museum in Baltimore, Maryland.

The good news is that if you're willing to put in the effort, a lot of other kids won't. Your knowledge and love of the sport will give you an edge over others. As in many endeavors in life few people have the work ethic it takes to persevere, and will quit at the first negative encounter, or when there is the least bit of resistance. Excuses are a part of their makeup. Remember this advice from me, "With excuses, no one's listening and no one cares. You either do it or you don't—and you pick it up and try it again." Millions of young people dream of major league careers, and there are only about seven hundred and fifty major leaguers at any one time, and less than three thousand professional players in the United States. But if you've got even a decent level of athleticism, combined with an outstanding work ethnic, you too can be one of them. Six-foot-five basketball players are a dime a dozen. But a six-foot-five baseball player who can run, hit, and throw is a marvel. In the 1970s, when Dave Parker and I were with the National League, we enjoyed being anomalies on the field: big athletic guys playing the game with five tools. Who wants to step up and fill those shoes today? You don't necessarily have to listen to everybody who tells you that your body size or shape makes you a better fit for a different sport. Bring your unusual strengths and skills to the game of baseball.

It's sad to say, but the obituary pages are full of football players who died before their time, or suffered permanent physical disabilities simply because of the toll the game took on their bodies. The competition for the impossibly small number of NBA jobs that open up in any given year is overwhelming. They only draft two rounds and many don't make it. Baseball players, by contrast, make the most money, have the longest careers, have the best pension and benefits, and can succeed even if they aren't considered the greatest all-around athletes.

Baseball is a game that rewards the thinker as much as it does the individual who has good reflexes. College coaches and major league managers prize the intelligent player, the one who is constantly willing to learn, the one who's constantly willing to improve his skills and sharpen his instincts. Kids, it's a great game. I don't know how else to put it. I hope that you'll follow in my footsteps and give it a try. You'll be glad you made the effort.

One final topic before I complete my discussion of kids and baseball: baseball cards. I must say that after signing my first contract, I felt a great deal of joy to see my first baseball card with my picture and information—even if I was in one of those hideous yellow uniforms from 1973. I'd still made it. As I said in my Hall of Fame speech, "If I'd have known I would've been this successful, I would have saved all my rookie cards!"

Not too long ago, I appeared at a baseball card show back East. Throughout the appearance, I was struck by the fact that there were more adults at the show than kids. Baseball cards used to be the purview of children, but no longer. Money changes everything. The marketing of baseball cards has become quite sophisticated and there are so many creative sets of cards available that kids no longer view cards as we did when I was a boy. Today, collectors sometimes don't even open the packs—that would ruin the cards' value. Baseball cards have become collectibles rather than artifacts of the game to be studied, traded, and enjoyed. While baseball cards are still the most collected of any sport, their true value now lies not in the individual owner's esteem of the cards, but in the card's monetary worth in the memorabilia business, eBay auctions, and projected appreciation values through Beckett and other publications. There has even been enough counterfeiting of baseball cards to demand an FBI intervention. Now there is a separate business strictly for authentication. The player, promoter, and card producer all get a cut. How could a kid afford a card under those circumstances?

When I was growing up, a baseball card was an entrée into the magical world of Major League Baseball, all for five cents. Back then, you got five cards and a stick of gum for a nickel. There was an element of surprise and excitement—you never knew who was inside that pack. Maybe it was a star from your favorite team, or a rookie card to stash away to see whether that player turned into something special. Maybe it was a coveted team-photo card, where you would study the faces of the players standing or sitting cross-legged on risers during spring training in some sun-drenched setting like Florida or Arizona. Or maybe it was the coveted checklist, which allowed you to identify which cards you had and which cards you needed to complete your set.

Back then, it wasn't possible to buy an entire set of baseball cards. But where was the fun in that? Why would you want to buy the entire set all at once? You would lose out on the serendipitous joy of coming across your favorite player next to that hard pink stick of gum, or winning several stars in a shrewd trade. Baseball cards eventually found their way into shoe boxes that you kept under your bed and hoped your mom wouldn't throw out. You acquired them slowly, and pursuit made them all the more valuable.

Baseball cards once offered you a free education in the vagaries of a professional ballplayer's career. You learned about geography and even history as you studied how a ballplayer's path wended from lower minor leagues and small towns to Double A and Triple A teams, until finally he reached a coveted spot in the majors. You studied his batting stance, high leg kick while pitching, and you imitated all your favorites in every pickup game you played. The first guy I followed was Zoilo Versalles of the Minnesota Twins. Because of him I learned to play shortstop.

When I was growing up, there were still plenty of ballplayers whose careers had been interrupted by the Korean War and World War II, and their baseball records, as memorialized on their baseball cards, indicated exactly what war service had interrupted their time spent in Major League Baseball. As an adult, I've been privileged to meet and befriend many of these true American heroes; guys who served in wartime like Yogi Berra, Jerry Coleman, Ted Williams, and Bob Feller.

In addition, you would spend endless hours studying the statistics available on the card. How many doubles had this player hit in his rookie year? His second year? His third? How many triples? Were his RBI totals moving up or down? If he was a pitcher, what was his ERA? His strikeout record? His record in the postseason?

This was well before the era of computer games and the Internet. We had more hours to while away, either studying baseball cards or playing baseball. At least back then, when you studied a baseball card, you learned a lot about baseball, and about life. The idea of one day being on your own baseball card was almost too exciting to even consider.

Baseball cards played an important role in the life of the typical American boy, and many an American girl. Baseball cards enticed kids to learn all they could about the game and thus to fall in love with it. The more you know about something, the more likely you are to embrace it deeply, and so it was with baseball for my friends and me. Basketball cards? Football cards? We might get them once in a while, but baseball cards were where it was at. We took our baseball cards everywhere—put them in the spokes of our bicycle wheels, tucked them into our waistbands, stuck them in our pockets, took them to bed, and hid them under our pillows, dreaming of the day that we might be major leaguers.

It's tough to have that kind of emotional connection to a baseball card today when it is stuck between Plexiglas or plastic. Kids treat baseball cards with a reverence that would have been unimaginable back in my day. They're afraid to even touch the things, lest oil from a thumbprint decrease the value of a Derek Jeter card from $2.50 down to a buck and a quarter.

You can't blame the card companies. They saw a need and they filled it, and they have been amply rewarded for doing so. The memorabilia craze really took off in the 1980s, and has continued unabated as new generations of kids have increasingly higher levels of allowance to spend. Nonetheless, at that card show, I saw few children, and I only saw one or two Hispanic individuals and only one African American young person, a girl about fourteen years of age. Kids have been priced out of the market for what is essentially a product made expressly for kids.

When kids see baseball cards as a vehicle for gaining wealth instead of a means of connecting to the game, it increases the alienation between players and fans. It used to be that if a kid wanted an autograph, he wanted it for himself. Today, he wants you to sign eight cards, and at least seven will be available on eBay before the final ball is pitched that evening.

Do I sign autographs when people ask? Of course I do, but not when people send them in the mail to my house. I consider it a privilege to be asked, and unless people are really annoying about it, I try to be gracious. I may not have played the game for a few years, but I still represent my sport and myself, and I intend to do it with grace and dignity whenever I am in the public eye or in a public place. Baseball fans have been very kind to me, so I'm simply trying to return the favor. But I will say that it gets frustrating when one person asks you to sign eight autographs, the majority of which you know are intended for resale.

Is there any way to turn back the hands of time with regard to baseball cards, and get them back in kids' pockets instead of those protective plastic sleeves? I doubt it. Our baseball cards might have gotten pretty ragged looking, and no collector would pay much for them today, but they meant everything to us, because they opened up the world of baseball.

Major League Baseball, seeking to capitalize on the still-booming collectibles market, recently created a new page on its website, www.mlb.com/cards. Here, the baseball card aficionado can find news and notes about baseball cards. I was curious about the intended audience for this site, so I clicked on a few of the offers for packs and card sets. In the first offering I clicked on, a full set of cards cost $84.95. I thought that might have been an aberration, so I clicked on a second offering. That one was $110. There aren't too many kids I know who can purchase baseball cards for that kind of money, especially since ordering over the Internet requires a credit card. Obviously, kids are not the intended audience for this site.

On top of that, the press release reporting the launching of the www.mlb.com/cards web page announced a special offer of collectible cards, and it gave kids the suggestion not to open the pack! Why would they tell kids that? Clearly, they want to advise kids to preserve the presumed high value of these special-offer cards. But you can't learn much about baseball from a card when it's still in its shrink wrap. If the whole point of baseball cards is to inform the youngest generation of potential fans about the history of the game, then there's a serious disconnect. Are we training the next generation of baseball fans, or the next generation of arbitrageurs?

I recently received an e-mail from a friend letting me know that my 1974 Topps rookie card, complete with authentication and advertised as one of only three in "10 Gem Mint" condition (whatever that means), was selling on eBay. It sold for $4,750. While I'm honored that someone would care to spend that much on my rookie baseball card (and please note that I don't see a dime from that transaction), the incident exemplifies what I'm talking about. That card seems destined for the bank deposit box, where no child will ever get to handle it. What's wrong with this picture? For me, the good news is that people consider my card a collectible . . . and not an antiquity!

CHAPTER 15

Baseball in the Twenty-first Century

Baseball has given me so much. It took a kid from the streets of St. Paul, Minnesota, gave me a dream, a vision of a career and a life, and allowed me to play the game I love before millions of fans for a long time. I am truly blessed and privileged. Along the way, I got a college education and fulfilled my boyhood dreams—and made a great living doing so. I am fortunate to have had the privileges of going directly to San Diego in the major leagues out of college; wearing Yankee pinstripes; playing for my home team, the Minnesota Twins; experiencing the triumph of winning a World Series in Toronto and being a hero to the entire nation of Canada; traveling the world; receiving the profound honor of having my number 31 retired (in one city); being elected the first year I was eligible to the National Baseball Hall of Fame; and most recently, being inducted into the Inaugural Class of the College Baseball Hall of Fame. That's just in the sport. I want to be known and remembered for being a leader not only on the field, but also in the community, giving back not only with money, but also with ideas, advocacy, time, and action.

I am extremely grateful for what baseball has done for me, and it is my fervent hope and dream that baseball has the chance to provide these same amazing opportunities to people and cities across North and South America, and around the world, and to generations of ballplayers to come. I want my legacy in sports, and to my kids and family, to be more than a plaque in Cooperstown, a World Series ring, or an entry in the baseball encyclopedia, as important and as dear as I hold each of those things.

The time is right, the opportunity is there, and I feel I have what it takes to create some action for a most worthwhile institution. What baseball means to America is tremendous. It is a shame to see it decline. We can really make a difference by having vision, commitment, determination, and using our resources intelligently and correctly. I want my gift to the game to be the fact that I helped change the course of the way we view baseball and the way that each of baseball's constituencies views their own responsibilities to this wonderful game.

One the of most hotly debated statistics in all of baseball is the "save." A save is awarded to a pitcher who comes in at the end of a baseball game and gets the final outs in situations where his team is winning by less than three runs.

The statistic is so hotly debated because a pitcher can come in, have a terrible performance and give up a few runs, thereby jeopardizing the win, and then get bailed out by a superior fielding play, thus securing the save for his statistics. Is that fair? Is that right? Maybe the center fielder crashing the wall and pulling a home-run ball back into the stadium ought to be the one who gets the save. Why should a pitcher who all but lost the game for his team be singled out for special credit? The same goes for the all-important rally to win the game. The entire team, and each of its participants, is important, whether he's the igniter who reaches first, then steals a base, or the guy who drives in the go-ahead run.

It shouldn't matter who gets the credit, who gets the "save" for remedying baseball's problems, or who starts or culminates the game-winning rally, as long as at the end of the day there is a win. They say the easiest way to get something done is to let other people take or share the credit. Just as there's no shortage of blame to pass around for the problems that baseball suffers today, there will be no shortage of credit and praise to pass around should baseball get back on track.

Baseball United is a campaign to turn baseball around, which is something I think just about everybody can feel good about. As we've discussed in each of the previous chapters, the game of baseball is a team effort extending far beyond the field. From the legends of the game to the kid breaking in his first mitt, baseball truly belongs to everyone. That's why we all have a responsibility to restore it.

The game I love *is* hurting, and I hope I've demonstrated the depth and the dimensions of that hurt. We're not talking about a situation that is beyond remedy. Baseball isn't a national joke along the lines of professional wrestling, although if it doesn't clean up its act and become more forward thinking and inclusive, and if it doesn't begin working together at the top and start exhibiting consistent leadership with integrity, the comparisons to wrestling won't be that long in coming. Baseball is a game of subtlety and beauty, and yet these joys are all too often pushed to the side by scandal, labor strife, and general neglect. Often issues are acted on after the horse is out of the barn, so to speak. What I've sought to do in this book is to share the deep concerns that I carry every day as I think about the game I love, and to offer you ways to get involved with its redemption and regeneration.

I'm trying to implement some of those recommendations with the MLB club I work with. We've had some success, but it's only a step. We need it on a bigger scale—from baseball's own leaders from MLB and MLBPA, from the cities and communities, and from the government and corporate America. Now is the time to stand up and do something.

I've written this book as a manifesto for change, and I hope my readers in the offices of Major League Baseball and the commissioners, the Players Association, the players themselves, and interested individuals and organizations elsewhere will recognize their responsibilities to lead this parade. Baseball United—by whatever name you might wish to call it—must be a top-down movement, embracing and leading the way for all. There is no reason not to embark upon this journey starting now. I'll be out there, publicly pushing for it.

After a recent collective-bargaining agreement, labor and management contributed $10 million to create an "Industry Growth Fund" for the purpose of expanding the popularity of baseball along with the fans' interest, thereby increasing industry growth in the twenty-first century. Players and owners *are* taking steps together. I urge them to continue to take some of the steps I've outlined publicly here, and others we've discussed privately.

The beautiful thing about baseball, the people's game, is that there is a place for everyone in society to participate. There's a role—and a responsibility—for all of us in restoring baseball's legacy, as long as the leadership is there. If you know me, you know how much I love baseball, and if you've only gotten to know me through this book, I'm certain that my love of the game has shone through on each and every page.

This book has been about the soul of the game, the underpinnings, the characteristics that have made baseball great. I hope that I have inspired you to ask, "How can I be a part of this? What's *my* role in Baseball United?"

The first step toward meaningful change is to honestly discern what the problems are. I've tried to be as frank as possible, laying out the issues and concerns that the game faces. But it wouldn't be constructive to just point a finger and pass the blame—as is all too often done in countless interviews and on talk shows. Instead, I've offered specific suggestions about what baseball can do to right its own ship, and ways in which everyone can contribute. Let's all work together to nab that save or get a big hit to help us win. Let's turn it around. Together, let's all play ball!

The Baseball United Plan

- The commissioner, the offices of Major League Baseball, the MLB Players Association, and all MLB players should make their top priority the creation of good relations between the owners and players for the ongoing benefit of the game and the fans.

- The commissioner, the offices of MLB, along with the Players Association and all MLB players, should collaborate in making Baseball United a reality (through collective bargaining and quiet, backstage diplomacy).

- Both camps should act with greater transparency and in good faith in their dealings with each other. They should take steps to put behind them the unpleasant, mistrustful relationship that has characterized labor-management disputes over the past three and a half decades, and instead adopt a spirit of unity, for the good of the game.

- Team owners should spend money to make baseball more readily available for kids throughout their territory, so as to compete for "mind share" with other sports, video games, extreme sports, skateboarding, etc.

- Team owners should make greater use of past and current players as ambassadors for the game in the ballpark and in the community, and make sure that the average fan has access to the players.

- Baseball should address the fact that those caught abusing steroids and performance-enhancing drugs are young players from both the U.S. and Latin American countries, and should find better ways to communicate its antidrug policies in all represented nations.

- Baseball should create Jackie Robinson Grants, in conjunction with corporate sponsors, players, and the NCAA, to provide financial assistance to deserving inner-city youths who may receive partial baseball scholarships in order to close the financial gap and allow them to attend school, thereby making baseball competitive with sports such as basketball and football.

- Baseball should offer awards, cash grants, and greater access to local organizations that bring baseball to lower-income communities, so as to call attention to those groups and permit their "best practices" to inspire others.

- Using the MLB Urban Youth Academy premises, baseball should create a mentoring program for all interested college baseball players, to match them with current and former major leaguers who can provide guidance about what it takes to make it in the major leagues.

- Players need to recognize a greater responsibility to give back to their hometowns and the communities where they play. Whether it's for one season or their entire careers, players are the true face of the game and baseball's most important and enduring asset. Remember, it's a privilege to play MLB.

You are not entitled to everything without the obligation of responsibility.

- Ownership should stop using the media as a tool for bashing the players prior to and during contract negotiation periods. The media outlet should be used to promote player importance to the game and to maintain the Baseball United campaign.

- Sports agents should recognize the authority they have and encourage players to take a more active role in their communities of origin, the cities in which they play, and in Baseball United as a whole.

- Leadership for Baseball United should come from MLB, the commissioner, and the Players Association—not from the corporate sector or government.

- If the right plan and leadership is present, then major corporate sponsors and institutions can affiliate themselves with Baseball United.

- Small businesses, neglected in recent decades, can sponsor the campaign at a lower level and teams can funnel income from them into community partnerships to build, refurbish, and staff baseball facilities in their areas.

- Parents should commit to "cleaning up their act" in every aspect of youth sports and set a better example for their children.

- Parents have to make time to get their kids to practice, play outdoors, eat healthfully, and be active, not just drive the kids to games.

- Parents need to find time to play catch with their kids and drag them away from electronic entertainment, to instill better physical-fitness habits.

- Parents need to know where to find organized baseball for young people, and to know where their kids can best develop their abilities.

- The MLB should contribute toward training youth coaches and umpires and seeking out more people to coach and officiate in youth games.

- Major League Baseball needs to borrow from the "best practices" of the NBA's and NFL's community-outreach and marketing programs to create more awareness of how baseball contributes to society.

- MLB should find corporate sponsors to help market and promote the game and its "cool factor," and find stars from other segments of society to help with awareness and increase its popularity.

- Baseball needs to take advantage of its ability to connect generations, by offering Generations Days, Family Reunion Days, Legends Games, and other special events at all major and minor league stadiums.

- MLB should create a database of all living Negro League players and share this information with its teams so that they can create special events to honor Negro League players and Negro League history and to connect them with present-day players and fans. This should be a permanent annual event at all ballparks.

  After Buck O'Neil passed away, it occurred to me that we

at the Padres could have honored him by giving him a one-day contract as a Major League Baseball player. And then I realized that any major league team could do the same for Negro League players alive today. Even at today's exalted minimum salaries, every baseball team could afford a one-day contract for the Negro Leaguers who were shut out of the majors when they were young. Major League Baseball, here's your opportunity to make things right for an entire generation. In their lifetimes, they will have made it to the big leagues.

You can think of the Negro League players as baseball's equivalent of the Greatest Generation. And like our World War II veterans, they will not be with us forever. A one-day contract will be a thrill of a lifetime for the Negro Leaguers and an unforgettable history lesson and community event for the rest of us.

- MLB teams should bring back and utilize local retired players and Hall of Famers to serve as ambassadors at the games, especially on promotional days.

- The NCAA should mandate a certain number of interviews for candidates of color for every baseball head coaching position at its member colleges and universities and develop closer bonds with the MLB Urban Academies and their contemplated showcase games, to further opportunities for urban and African American ballplayers.

- A business website should be created that provides accurate, impartial information about ethnically diverse, underprivileged, and inner-city junior high and high school players, thus bringing them to the attention of college baseball recruiting officials who might not otherwise have access to information about these players.

- A study should be undertaken to find out why there are so few African American players and coaches at the collegiate level and to find ways to work with the NCAA to remedy this situation, since colleges and universities are the primary means by which American baseball players reach the major leagues.

- Let's honor the generosity and contributions of today's youth coaches more publicly and more often.

- Baseball should provide uniformly high levels of training to coaches and referees at all levels of youth baseball, taking advantage of major and minor league personnel and using their facilities across the nation as training centers.

- Coaches should know how to make practices interesting and exciting for today's generation of kids, so that they maintain interest. They should attend continuing-education seminars and preview the latest videos. Read up, coaches. Even old dogs can learn new (and necessary) tricks.

- Coaches should know about opportunities for players to advance in their training, and get more exposure and preparation, including traveling teams, college camps and clinics, and showcase games.

- Coaches need to know about the specific training and conditioning needs (equipment, centers, food, and nutrition) for the benefit of their baseball players.

- Major League Baseball should create partnerships with the AARP (whose members are fifty years old or older), Volunteers of America, and other nationwide volunteer organizations to find new youth coaches.

- Kids need to recognize that a career in baseball may be more likely for them than a career in the NBA or NFL. Compare and contrast the pros and cons of all, including the health benefits associated with each.

- Kids should spend more time practicing their skills and less time playing computer games. Start with a wall, a ball, and your glove.

- Kids need to ignore those who tell them that if they're tall they can only play basketball or if they're stocky they're "built" for football. Any body type can make it in baseball.

- Kids can ask their parents and grandparents about games like stickball and strikeout, stoopball, over-the-line, and home-run derby, which require only a bare minimum of financial investment and only a few other players, but which provide a wealth of opportunity to improve skills.

- Local lawmakers should pass stricter laws and legislation to keep convicted child molesters and predators at a distance from playgrounds and recreational areas.

- Government on all levels can play an important role in making baseball available in inner cities and economically depressed areas by providing tax benefits to companies that create baseball fields and leagues in those places.

Acknowledgments

I would like to acknowledge my parents, my coaches, the recreation system of St. Paul, the University of Minnesota, the Padres, Yankees, Angels, Blue Jays, Twins, and Indians. Thank you, Paul Fedorko, of Trident Media Group, my outstanding literary agent, for your professionalism and thoroughness in making this book a reality. I would also like to recognize Terrie Barna for her wonderful work typing the original manuscript, along with Jenna Rose Robbins, Eugenia Chung, Nicole Rhoton, Heather Riccio, Ragnhild Hagen, and Kathleen Rizzo for their meticulous efforts in copyediting and working on the book. A special thanks to my editor, Brant Rumble, and Anna DeVries for all their hard work.